Introducing APEL

Further education: the assessment and accreditation
of prior learning series
Edited by Norman Evans and Michèle Bailleux, both
of the Learning from Experience Trust

Introducing APEL

Maggie Challis

London and New York

First published 1993
by Routledge
11 New Fetter Lane

Transferred to Digital Printing 2004

Simultaneously published in the USA and Canada
by Routledge
29 West 35th Street, New York, NY 10001

Typeset in Palatino by LaserScript, Mitcham, Surrey

British Library Cataloguing in Publication Data
A catalogue reference for this book is available from the British Library

ISBN 0–415–09244–2

Library of Congress Cataloging in Publication Data
has been applied for.

ISBN 0–415–09244–2

Contents

Figures and tables

Series Editors' foreword to
Introducing APEL

Much current interest and development in colleges and training organisations is concerned with the accreditation of prior learning in relation to its application alongside work-based assessment and assessment on demand. However, well before National Vocational Qualifications came on the scene, with their powerful impetus behind such concern, there was already a movement towards helping people identify the unrecognised learning and the many skills they had acquired outside paid work and in domestic and voluntary work. This process was termed the Accreditation of Prior Experiential Learning (APEL) and it remains a priority for those professionals concerned with helping individuals return to education or work at a pace and level appropriate to their real learning, rather than simply those aspects that have already been certificated or otherwise recognised, or can be recognised through assessment on demand.

This book examines the history and applications of APEL, and sets them in the current legislative, educational and training environment. It shows the role of APEL as a means of facilitating access to education, training and work, through relating learning from experience to the desired targets of the individual. In some cases this may be a National Vocational Qualification – the process currently termed the Accreditation of Prior Learning – but in others it is simply entry to a course of study or a successful job application. Its leitmotif is access for adults.

The book concentrates principally on how to work through the APEL process with individuals, and points to the necessity for an open and flexible structure in colleges to facilitate its implementation. It therefore serves as an admirable vanguard for Mike Field's book *APL: Developing Flexible Colleges*.

Introducing APEL is a book designed for practitioners, written by a practitioner, and contains many valuable case studies and checklists which tutors and managers alike may draw on in developing good practice within their own institutions.

Norman Evans, Director, Learning from Experience Trust
Michèle Bailleux, Deputy Director Learning from
Experience Trust
London 1992

Foreword to the series

In Britain, the assessment and accreditation of prior learning (APL) began with the assessment of prior experiential learning (APEL). When discussion first began about APEL and further education, accreditation of anything other than examined outcomes was hardly on the map. Partly this was because APEL was seen as an additional way of widening access. But also it was because self-assessment stood out as one of the richest dividends for individuals from APEL. Accreditation might follow, but that was a separate issue. Over time, and that means from the early 1980s, the term APL has come to refer to all previously acquired learning, which necessarily includes experiential learning. So whereas APEL refers specifically to uncertificated learning, APL refers to that as well as to previous learning that has been formally certificated through some recognised examining body. Both are vital. So often the one can lead to the other and both can serve as approach routes to additional formal learning. Throughout the books in this series, this distinction needs to be borne in mind. Perhaps the easiest way is to think of APEL as a subset of APL. And now, of course, accreditation is a lively issue for both.

Discussions about introducing the assessment of prior experiential learning to formal education in Britain began with higher education in the early 1980s. About two years later, further education entered the arena in two ways. Jack Mansell, then Chief Officer of the Further Education Unit, commissioned a project which resulted in the publication in 1984 of *Curriculum Opportunity: a map of experiential learning in entry requirements to higher and further education award-bearing courses*. Alun Davies, then the Chief Inspector for Higher and Further Education in the Inner London Education Authority, recognised the potential of APEL for further education as an influence on curriculum reform, staff development and for assisting colleges to prepare for a future that was going to be different from the past and present. So he gave a brief to a succession of enthusiastic and energetic staff in the Curriculum Development Unit to promote APEL activities in colleges wherever they could.

As some staff moved on to other posts inside and outside London, APEL activities spread so that by the time the National Council for Vocational Qualifications was established in 1986, there were staff in a number of further education colleges who had gone some way towards developing schemes for APEL, some of them promoted by the FEU, some of them connected with REPLAN projects for the unemployed. The Unit for the Development of Adult and Continuing Education took a hand through its programme of work on Access. And as Open College Federations and Networks worked at ways of awarding official recognition to non-institutional, off-campus learning, so they added yet another strand to APEL activities. As the benefits of progression and credit accumulation began to be more widely appreciated, both APL and APEL became an increasingly important dimension to Access, while NCVQ gave a strong lead in that direction through its own version of Prior Learning Achievements.

Now colleges face a different and uncertain future. It seems that to remain effective as incorporated institutions, they have to find ways of supplementing their funding from the FEFC, while pursuing policies designed to increase and widen participation. That means evolving imaginative forms of collaboration with industry and commerce. It means finding viable ways of handling Vocational Qualifications. And it all poses difficult organisational issues for a college that sets out to meet that range of requirements. So APL and APEL have become deadly serious considerations, so much so that it would be hard work to walk into any college without finding people who were talking about both. And often at the heart of those discussions there is the tension between using both APL and APEL for personal development and as a component of liberal education and seeing them as part of the provision for Vocational Qualifications.

In the real world of day-to-day activity in colleges, however, there is more talk than action. This is not surprising. Incorporating APL as a mainstream activity rather then seeing it as something rather fancy at the margins, touches issues from the top to the bottom of any institution. Overall management, academic organisation, the curriculum, modes of learning, teaching styles and delivery, admissions, student guidance and support systems, assessment procedures, relations with awarding bodies and NCVQ and, more recently, with higher education through franchising and associated status, all come into the reckoning. And since, as the books in this series imply, flexibility needs to be the hallmark of successful colleges in the future, and the effective introduction of APL requires flexibility, the message is clear. Colleges need APL to be flexible, effectively. APL requires flexibility to be successful within an institution.

This series of books on Further Education: the Assessment and Accreditation of Prior Learning, is a contribution towards encouraging colleges to incorporate APL schemes as mainstream provision. Moreover, we hope that because each of these books is written by men and women who know what they are talking about from their direct professional experience in the theory and practice of APL and APEL, whatever the particular focus of their writing, they will be of practical help to colleges and college staff wishing to develop schemes of their own.

Norman Evans, Director, Learning from Experience Trust
Michèle Bailleux, Deputy Director, Learning from
Experience Trust
London, 1992

Abbreviations

AAPLA	Assessment and Accreditation of Prior Learning and Achievement
ACC	Accreditation of Current Competence
APA	Accreditation of Prior Achievement
APEL	Accreditation of Prior Experiential Learning
APL	Accreditation of Prior Learning/Assessment of Prior Learning
APLA	Accreditation of Prior Learning and Achievement
BTEC	Business and Technology Education Council
CATS	Credit Accumulation and Transfer Schemes
CGLI	City and Guilds of London Institute
GNVQ	General National Vocational Qualification
HE	Higher Education
ILB	Industry Lead Body
IPEL	Identifying Prior Experiential Learning
LEC	Local Enterprise Company
NCVQ	National Council for Vocational Qualifications
NIACE	National Institute of Adult Continuing Education
NVQ	National Vocational Qualifications
OCN	Open College Network
PLA	Prior Learning Assessment
RPL	Recognising Prior Learning
SVQ	Scottish Vocational Qualification
TDLB	Training and Development Lead Body
TEC	Training and Enterprise Council
VQ	Vocational Qualification
YTS	Youth Training Scheme

Chapter 1

The Accreditation of Prior Experiential Learning

A historical context

WHAT IS APEL?

The fundamental principle underpinning the Accreditation of Prior Experiential Learning is that learning is worthy and capable of gaining recognition and credit, regardless of the time, place and context in which it has been achieved. It thus represents a move to accept that learning is not dependent upon any particular formal setting, and to acknowledge it as being of value in its own right.

The fact that learning accumulates and exists outside an education or training environment cannot be disputed. Yet it is traditionally only institutional, certificated learning that carries any status. Uncertificated learning – such as that gained during a period of employment, or partial completion of a course of study, or during voluntary or unpaid work – is acknowledged, informally, as being somehow useful or valuable, but until now, there has never been an attempt to quantify the learning that has taken place.

The result of this informal acknowlegement of prior learning has been exemption or advanced standing given to learners on the basis of a rough rule of thumb (and often linked to viable numbers needed to run a course). However, this process does not put a value on the learning: it simply acknowledges that it exists. The Accreditation of Prior Experiential Learning seeks to give positive credit for all learning, by placing it within a recognised accreditation framework.

In brief, then, APEL involves:

- the identification of learning, wherever and whenever this has taken place

- the selection of that learning which is relevant to a desired outcome or progression route
- demonstration of the validity and appropriateness of this learning
- matching learning outcomes to those stated within a chosen accreditation or progression framework
- assessment of evidence against predetermined criteria to ensure the validity of the claimed competence
- accreditation within an appropriate accreditation framework.

The notion of learning from experience is, of course, nothing new. For generations, apprentices and initiates into almost any trade learned by 'sitting next to Nellie'. Bit by bit they acquired that experience and knowledge that enabled them to become recognised as craftspersons in their own right. Yet in educational circles, such practical learning has generally been considered somehow inferior to book learning, which has always been seen as the key to 'success' – usually measured in terms of a combination of status and money.

The current interest in the application of learning from experience, in academic as well as workplace pursuits, originated in the United States of America in the 1970s. During the middle decades of the century, the work of philosophers and psychologists such as Dewey, Locke, Piaget and, from the 1970s, Kolb and others drew attention to the particular needs of adult learners and appropriate learning styles for them. It was perhaps inevitable that from this would grow an education system that takes into account the main difference between older and younger learners – the fact that they have been out in the world, and have learned a lot as a result. The result, in America, was that a research project was set up in Princeton, New Jersey, to investigate the potential use of prior learning for entry to higher education. This was done by trying to equate non-college learning to the curriculum offered in colleges and to establish a reliable methodology for its assessment. The results indicated the feasibility of such an approach.

As so often happens, interest spread across the Atlantic and, as a result, a series of exchange visits took place between the United States and Britain during the early 1980s. Again, there was particular emphasis on adults seeking entry into higher education. Originally supported by the Policy Studies Institute, interest in the whole area of work grew and became espoused by the Further

Education Unit, the Council for National Academic Awards, and the (then) Manpower Services Commission. Each brought to bear on the subject its own particular emphasis. Throughout all these developments, the voice of the Learning from Experience Trust has consistently been heard keeping the issue alive across the whole gamut of contexts in which the Accreditation of Prior Experiential Learning is, or could be, of relevance.

In addition to the work of the Learning from Experience Trust, APEL has been brought to wider attention and given credibility by the development of National Vocational Qualifications. These define and describe vocational competence, which is assessed by outcome. The time, place or context in which this competence has been gained is irrelevant to the assessment of the competence. Thus gaining credit for past learning and achievement becomes a real possibility.

In 1986 the Government established the National Council for Vocational Qualifications (NCVQ), with the broad aims, stated in the Government's 'Working Together – Education and Training' (Cmnd 9823, July 1986) of

- effecting an improvement in vocational qualifications by basing them on the standards of competence required in employment
- establishing a National Vocational Qualification (NVQ) framework which is comprehensible, comprehensive and facilitates access, progress and continued learning.

These qualifications are built on a structure of units and elements and arranged in a hierarchy of levels, ranging from competence in routine tasks under supervision at Level 1, to autonomous postgraduate competence at Level 5. This structure facilitates, and indeed encourages, the Accreditation of Prior Experiential Learning, as learners can build towards a qualification at a time, pace and level that is appropriate to their needs and current competence. (See Appendix 1 for structure of NVQs.) The intention was, on the creation of the NCVQ, that by the end of 1992, competences should be described that fall within the grasp of 80 per cent of the British workforce. Although still not complete, the NVQ framework is now largely in place.

And so it came to be that the concept born of philosophical and psychological origins, and adopted by American educators, became transported across the Atlantic, to reappear in Britain as an integral part of a new rationalisation of vocational education and training.

As with most novelties, the concept of APEL has acquired a vocabulary and jargon of its own. Not least among these is the plethora of acronyms used to refer to the process:

APEL this acronym, standing for the Accreditation of Prior Experiential Learning, makes explicit the notion of learning from experience. It is one that is much favoured by those practitioners who choose to place emphasis on the process of identifying skills acquired, particularly in non-vocational settings, as much as on the end product of accreditation. It is this version that will be used throughout this book.

APL the most common and probably most generally recognised in further education, is the Employment Department preferred model. It stands, simply, for the Accreditation of Prior Learning, and has been the focus of a series of development projects run by the Employment Department, Training and Enterprise Councils (TECs) and further education colleges.

APL confusingly, this version is also used for the Assessment of Prior Learning, which describes a process in which learning is identified and assessed, but may not be submitted for final accreditation, or where the assessment has not been carried out for the qualification currently being sought.

APA and APLA the Accreditation of Prior Achievement and the Accreditation of Prior Learning and Achievement. Both these have been used mainly by awarding bodies, and the tendency has been to interpret them both as using evidence of previously recognised learning – for example certificates – in order to gain credit towards an NVQ.

AAPLA not used often, but this relates to the Assessment and Accreditation of Prior Learning and Achievement. Although perhaps the most accurate and all-embracing, this version does not seem set to become mainstream.

ACC Arising from the apparent need to find a simple definition of what the whole process is really about, the latest acronym to hit the stage is this one – standing for the Accreditation of Current Competence. This shift from past learning to present ability reflects the concern of many educators, trainers and awarding bodies, which is: How prior is 'prior' learning? Does achievement need a defined shelf-life in order to decide whether it is to be seen as valid, or is the easiest way to judge its credit-worthiness simply to reassess against current criteria? This version of the current acronyms may be an accurate description of the end of the process for those who seek 'hard' accreditation, but it seems to lose something by reducing the emphasis on learning or achievement that needs to be identified before the assessment of current competence can be undertaken.

The common thread that binds all these together is the assessment of learning achievement, both current and prior, regardless of time, place, or method of its achievement. APEL is distinctive in that it seeks to accredit non-certificated prior learning that is experiential.

Whilst on the subject of acronyms, perhaps it would be helpful, for the sake of completeness, to say that the standard form now used in the USA is PLA – Prior Learning Assessment – and the emerging interest in the subject in Australia is working to the RPL acronym – Recognising Prior Learning.

The British model is able to offer not only recognition and assessment, but also accreditation in a very practical and tangible sense in terms of certificates. This began first in higher education as academic credit towards diplomas, bachelors and masters degrees, and has since expanded to different areas, partly through the development of the unit-based framework of National Vocational Qualifications and other developing initiatives that seek to award credit for demonstrated learning within a context of clearly specified outcomes.

WHERE CAN APEL BE USED?

The early 1990s have seen an extraordinarily fast rise in interest in APEL. In fact, the high profile that has been given to the concept, mainly through Government-funded research and implementation projects, has led to the impression in some areas that APEL is the key to a redesigned, student-centred, Post-16 education system. In many ways, this can be seen to be the case. The rationale behind APEL does place the learner, rather than the course or learning programme, very firmly at the centre of operations. However, it is important to say that APEL is merely one of a range of tools for assessment available to colleges and other education and training providers. It therefore needs to be seen alongside other forms of formative and summative assessment that take place from the learner's first contact with the college or training establishment, during induction and attendance, and on exit from the institution.

Because it is totally individual, APEL is one of the most student-centred activities in which colleges can engage. It relies on a process of exploring and identifying skills and competence, and, if appropriately supported, this will inevitably lead to increased confidence in the learner. The assessment and accreditation of what is revealed through this process takes place against criteria that are known to the learner, and against which suitable evidence of competence has been prepared and matched. The process is therefore one of empowerment, and makes the concept of 'failure' irrelevant. The process is non-competitive, because each learner's experience and learning is different from any other's. Thus each account of documented evidence of learning created by learners, sometimes in the form of a portfolio, is distinct and personal. It is obvious that this is a totally different process from the traditional teach-and-test environment of the old-style further and higher education provision.

The empowering and individual nature of the APEL process and its potential application across a wide range of learning contexts has meant that it has been used by practitioners from all areas of education and training.

Assessors for NVQs use APEL to enable learners to claim units of competence against occupational standards or national qualifications.

Case study 1.1

Angela

Angela left school at 16 and went on to a clerical Youth Training Scheme. At the end of her course, she had done a single-subject typing exam, and had acquired a good understanding of the theory and practice of office work. She applied for, and was appointed to, a general administrative post, where she heard of the possibility of using her prior learning and current work practice to claim a qualification.

She went to her local college, and was referred to a tutor who gave her an in-depth interview in order roughly to assess the level and range of her ability. The tutor was convinced that Angela could claim the major part of the RSA Diploma in Office Procedures, and showed her the list of tasks involved. (This qualification has now been replaced by the NVQ Level 2 in Business Administration.) On a first read-through, Angela felt sure she could meet the requirements in most of the tasks. However, she did not in her present work undertake planning and booking procedures, and she did not currently have any role in handling finance or dealing with wages and salaries.

The college tutor suggested to Angela that there might be areas outside work where she could find evidence to prove she could carry out these tasks. Did she, for example, book holidays for herself and friends. Did she have a bank account with a cheque book? Did she pay any of her bills by credit transfer or direct debit? On reflection, Angela was able to identify, with the help of her tutor, places where she could gather evidence for almost all the tasks.

She was given a copy of the tasks, and a checklist for her line manager at work to sign as additional evidence of Angela's competence at work. She was able to negotiate with her employer to spend some time in the finance section in order to gain the additional experience needed in her 'weak' area.

At the end of the day, Angela gained the diploma, without having to attend a single college class. In addition to the qualification, however, she had learned a great deal about herself, related her non-work activities to a potential vocational role, and had not only negotiated an appropriate learning method for herself, but also learned how to use her colleagues and her workplace as a source of learning.

Case study 1.2

Keith

Admissions tutors address a learner's prior learning and experience through a process of initial counselling and guidnance in order to identify appropriate learning programmes and/or give exemption from parts of those programmes.

Keith was a 37-year-old man who had applied for a four-year BSc in Industrial Studies. He came to the attention of the local Polytechnic CATS unit because he was seeking exemption from the sandwich year on the degree on the basis of his many years of relevant employment (both technical and commercial) in industry. Discussions revealed that Keith already had an HNC in Electrical Engineering, and as a result of both formal training and experience, he also had a considerable amount of technical and managerial competence.

The course team was persuaded to recognise the HNC as being worth 60 credit points at Level 1 (equivalent to half of the first year). A programme was designed for Keith to follow which was made up of first- and second-year units. It was agreed that if Keith appeared to be successfully coping with the formal course of study, he should present a claim for the equivalent of the remaining two second-year units on the basis of his prior uncertificated learning.

Keith proved to be an excellent student. He applied for permission to make a claim for APEL. The initial appraisal suggested a few minor gaps in his knowledge which could easily be made up by directed reading. Keith had difficulty providing documentary evidence, so he asked for his portfolio to be supplemented by written assignments set by the assessors. He was able to demonstrate that he had achieved the desired learning outcomes, and was allowed to proceed to the final year. He should now achieve the degree in two years instead of the original four.

Case study 1.3

Louise

Access to higher education programmes incorporate APEL as a means of increasing the confidence of adult learners in their ability to contribute to their present or future learning environment.

Louise was one of a number of nurse tutors who approached the local polytechnic following the changes in nursing education brought about by Project 2000. She, like many of her colleagues, had been involved in developing and delivering courses to student nurses which had been credit-rated at Level 2 (i.e. second-year degree level). Unfortunately, because nothing else had been available for her, Louise herself had accumulated a large amount of credit at Level 1 (first-year degree level). Ironically, on completion of her course, Louise's students were better qualified than she was!

In order to continue in her employment, Louise was required to obtain a degree. On the basis of her certificated learning, she would probably have been allowed straight on to Level 2 of the Diploma in Professional Studies in Nursing. This would still have meant four years of part-time study in order to achieve a degree. Following an interview, Louise was made an offer of a place on a new, two-year, 'top-up degree' primarily designed for students who already had a diploma. This offer was conditional on her satisfactorily achieving 120 Level 2 points through APEL.

Louise was not seeking to match exactly any existing course, so had to package her learning into sensible learning components which could then be credit-rated as if they were a taught course. The initial assessment supported the view that Louise did have the basis for a claim for 120 Level 2 points, and she was allowed to proceed.

Candidates at the polytechnic are also required to describe how they achieved the learning outcomes as well as provide evidence of their achievement. Louise's claim was particularly effective in this respect, and this, together with the quality of her documentary support, meant that the assessors did not find it necessary to set additional assessments. Louise was one of six candidates who obtained places on that particular top-up degree as a result of an APEL claim.

Case study 1.4

Aisha

Tutors of learners with a range of special and individual needs find APEL provides a vehicle for people of all ages and backgrounds to examine their learning needs, based on knowledge of where they have succeeded in the past.

Aisha came to Britain from Somalia in 1988. After leaving home in her own country, she started work in a travel agent, and also helped her mother run a clothing stall in the local market. Although a superb seamstress and embroiderer, she did not value her talents in this area as it was something that was expected of her at home, and therefore unexceptional.

When she came to England, she had no English, no income and two small children. She joined a lunch club run by and for Somali women. A support worker with the club encouraged Aisha and the other women to analyse their skills and look at positive ways in which they could use them. With the help of a counsellor and a bilingual member of the group, Aisha came to recognise her many abilities and explore areas in which she could put them to good use. Aisha was eventually able to negotiate a contract for herself and other group members with a local branch of a Third World trading organisation, to whom they are selling their garments and other artefacts.

Case study 1.5

John

Adult education tutors use the process of creating a portfolio of experience and learning to help learners develop a sense of their own value and open doors to future education, training or employment.

John had been made redundant twice in three years. The first time, he lost a job in manufacturing, while the second time, the Employment Training Scheme he was managing had its funding reduced, resulting in the end of the scheme.

He attended a local job club, where he was encouraged to analyse his strengths, weaknesses and preferences for employment, and to build a portfolio based on an extended curriculum vitae. During this process, it was revealed that John was also a magistrate and a school governor, but had tended to disregard these activities, seeing them as irrelevant to the search for jobs.

John's job club leader helped him think through all the skills that these community activities had helped him develop, and he created a profile of himself that was greatly different from the one he presented on first attending the job club. Consequently, the type of job he started applying for, and the way he presented himself in his applications, became much more positive, and he used evidence from his portfolio to support his claims to meet the job description. He is now working happily in a college, as a placement officer for young people with special educational needs undertaking work experience.

Case study 1.6

Ann

Ann gave up office work when she had her first child, and did no paid work until he reached school age. By that time Ann also had a daughter. She started to do a little child-minding from home, taking on two more pre-school children. Although she enjoyed the work, Ann did not want to spend the rest of her life looking after small children, but wanted more adult company. She did not really want to go back to the sort of work that she had done before.

As a first step to getting back to paid work outside her home, she joined a part-time word processing course at her local college, and also joined a women's group at one of the college's neighbourhood centres. In this group, she discovered that she was not the only person in her circumstances. An APEL counsellor was invited into the group to work with them for a few weeks on analysing their skills and thinking about planning for future work or training. Ann found the experience extremely helpful, and began to believe in her many skills and talents that had been developed during her time with her own and other people's children.

Within weeks, Ann applied for a job and was invited for interview. She told no one in the group what she was doing until after the event – just in case the whole thing fell flat. However, she was offered the first job she applied for, as a laboratory assistant in the local children's hospital. In addition, she was confident enough to negotiate flexible hours of work to minimise childcare costs for her own children after school. The job was exactly what she had hoped for,

involving work within a child-orientated, caring environment, and enabling her to use her personal qualities as a
highly organised and methodical worker.

Case study 1.7

Dave

The process of identifying the range of individual learning
has been used in redundancy counselling to help identify
appropriate training, retraining or employment prospects.

Dave worked for 22 years in a steel works, choosing to
stay in semi-skilled work on the plant instead of seeking
training and promotion, and put a lot of time and energy into
his role as shop steward. When the plant was threatened
with closure, he was instrumental in setting up redundancy
counselling for all the 240 men and 6 women about to lose
their jobs.

When his turn came to be counselled, he, like so many
of his colleagues, had no clear ideas about future work or
training. He intended to concentrate on his 'side line' –
buying, restoring and selling antiques. The redundancy
package on offer included the right to attend an approved
education or training course, and Dave was encouraged to
look at how he could combine his interest and his training
budget.

He went for a detailed interview at a college offering
courses in furniture restoration. With the help of a counsellor, he was able to list the skills and knowledge that he
had acquired in relation to antique furniture. As a result of
this, he was exempted from the first, college-based part of
the course, and sent straight on to work placement alongside one of the region's foremost renovators of antique
furniture.

The list of contexts in which APEL is being used is long and
growing. School-leavers now find that they can use their school
learning not only as a platform from which to enter college, but it

can actually be accredited towards a vocational qualification and give them exemption from parts of the next stage of their education. Research being carried out by the National Institute of Adult Continuing Education (NIACE) is investigating the transferability of outcomes demonstrated in professional qualifications gained overseas. All of these examples show the range and scope of the growing interest nationally in APEL.

WHAT APEL IS NOT

Having spent some time now saying what APEL is and how it can be used, it seems appropriate also to say what it is not.

APEL is not a means of giving 'credit for living'.

It is credit for learning. It is important to stress this, and stress it frequently. Without acknowledgement of this fact, APEL runs the risk of becoming marginalised at the edge of education and training, instead of taking up its rightful place in the centre.

APEL is not a quick and easy route for the learner to somehow get something for nothing.

The process of identifying and demonstrating learning for accreditation purposes is arduous, both emotionally and physically.

APEL is not necessarily a cheap option, either for learners or for providers.

In addition to the cost of certification, the learner may have to pay for the support needed during preparation of evidence of learning. In order to meet the individual needs of learners, institutions will have to divert funds away from traditional classroom-based activities into work with individuals and small groups. Whilst this may result in more satisfied customers, and quicker 'throughput' of learners, it will require investment in planning and preparation before it can be implemented.

APEL is not the most appropriate route for every learner.

By its very nature, following through APEL to its logical conclusion obviates the need for some learners to attend a programme of learning. Yet for many people, it is precisely the attendance at a learning institution, mixing with a new and varied peer group and being part of a communal process, that is most valuable. This in itself becomes part of the learning process and may be an aim in its own right.

However, it makes sound educational sense for every learner to be given the time and help necessary to identify prior learning, and make decisions as to the most appropriate route to build upon this. The counselling base of the APEL process should reveal the learning needs of the individual, and whether these are best met by attend- ance on a learning programme. Immediate accreditation will not necessarily be the desired outcome.

WHY IS APEL ATTRACTIVE TO LEARNERS?

Despite all the above provisos, there are increasing numbers of learners seeking accreditation through APEL rather than through a more traditional, taught route to a qualification. Probably the major reason for this is that APEL saves time and gives flexibility. Preparation of evidence of learning can be done at home, at work or in leisure pursuits. It can thus fit easily into normal routines. There is no commitment to a regular class at college which can be disruptive to routines and impossible to maintain for people with a fluid or changeable work pattern or domestic commitments. Equally, in order to gain a qualification that would otherwise require full-time study, there is no need to give up work, with all the emotional and financial burdens that this imposes.

Another reason is that, where some study is needed, there is a need to attend only those parts of a programme that are necessary for further certification or progression. One of the best ways to lose the interest of learners is to 'teach' them things they already know. Almost any course of study will contain some elements that are familiar to its members, and a little revision is usually not a bad thing. However, APEL affords a route whereby what has already been learned does not have to be relearned and retested. At the same time, it pinpoints areas for further development, which are crystallised in an action plan that has developed from a learner's individual learning profile.

Control of the APEL process lies firmly in the hands of the learner. The identification of learning, the preparation of evidence of learning, the presentation of this evidence, and the framework in which accreditation is sought all rest with the individual claimant. Thus the pace and timing of claims will vary from one person to another, as will the evidence of learning and the plan for progression. It is easy to see why this route is preferable for some people, as opposed to being part of a group for a predetermined period of time, with a fixed attendance pattern, where they are taught things with which they are already familiar, and are assessed on a once-for-all basis at the end of the programme of study.

WHY NOW?

Reference has already been made to the relevance, in terms of the development of APEL, of the introduction of NVQs. However, this is only one of a range of developments that have highlighted the appropriateness of APEL and made its implementation feasible and desirable. The world of education and training is in a state of flux, but all the present initiatives and directives are pointing to the need for a more learner-centred environment and one in which APEL becomes increasingly relevant.

Demographic trends

No examination of current changes in post-compulsory education can be complete without reference to one of the underlying causes of them all. The drop in the number of 16- to 19-year-olds in this country was foreseen as the great opportunity for adults to gain increased employment opportunities. It was perceived that there would be a need for employers to look for new sources for their employees as the supply of school-leavers dried up.

The recession has taken its toll on these hopes, and employment prospects have not blossomed as anticipated. Yet, despite the recession, there are still opportunities that did not exist ten years ago for older people to re-enter the work market. However, competition for jobs is intense, and the more evidence of experience that can be given to support an application, the better. This is especially true in cases where the applicant left school with no paper qualifications.

The appointment of mature applicants to vacant posts brings with it added benefits for employers. They are taking on people who may need little or no initial training – not only for the specific job role, but also for the underpinning 'core' skills of how to work as part of a team, how to communicate effectively, how to organise personal time, how to respond to the unexpected, how to engage in problem-solving. Adults, through their life experience, have many of these skills, but a period away from a work environment can lead to a loss of confidence.

The APEL process helps adults recognise and market their skills in such a way that they become highlighted not only for the individual, but also for any potential employer. A portfolio evidencing skills relevant to employment, and the context in which they have been gained, adds weight to an individual's claim to possessing them. In some cases, it has been possible to use this portfolio of evidence to gain the precise qualification being sought by employers for a particular job, thus giving an additional boost to the adult seeking work.

Government policy

In a series of White Papers and legislation, the Government has declared its intention to raise the profile of education and training through a series of measures:

> Unlocking the potential of individual people by giving them the chance to acquire skills and qualifications will be of the greatest importance in the years ahead. It will not only determine success and self-fulfilment for people themselves. It will also be essential to sustain a successful national economy in an increasingly competitive world.
>
> (HMSO 1992)

One of the measures adopted by the Government has been the creation of the Training and Enterprise Councils (TECs) in England and Wales and the Local Enterprise Companies (LECs) in Scotland in order to 'unlock the potential of individuals, companies and communities'. A principal aim of TECs and LECs is to raise the local skills base and promote economic and business growth and work towards the achievement of the National Education and Training targets. One of the ways in which their success will be measured is by the number and level of awards of National Vocational Qualifications (or Scottish Vocational Qualifications) within their area. One of their priorities is therefore to establish increased access to these qualifications. This is being done through net- works of local businesses, trainers, educators and assessors.

One of their first activities is to identify what skills and abilities already exist within the local community, in order for claims to competence in NVQs to be made, and for appropriate assessment and training to be made available for future development. This process in itself will be arduous as it involves not only establishing the networks, but also educating the local population about the possibilities open to them, and training employers to undertake some of the assessment processes.

However, it is clear that through TECs and LECs, the principle of lifelong education and training may reach those people who would not currently consider going to college. They will be able to have their competence assessed in the workplace or elsewhere, and use all their experience from home, work and community activities to build a personal path to a qualification and to possible promotion and career change.

National education and training targets

The publication by the Government of national education and training targets may equally provide a stimulus for the implementation of APEL. These targets are divided into Foundation and Lifetime Learning targets:

Foundation

1 By 1997, 80 per cent of young people to reach NVQ II (or equivalent)
2 Training and education to NVQ III (or equivalent) available to all young people who can benefit
3 By 2000, 50 per cent of young people to reach NVQ III (or equivalent)
4 Education and training provision to develop self-reliance, flexibility and breadth

Lifetime

1 By 1996, all employees should take part in training or development activities

2 By 1996, 50 per cent of the workforce aiming for NVQs or units
   towards them
3 By 2000, 50 per cent of the workforce qualified to at least NVQ
   III (or equivalent)
4 By 1996, 50 per cent of medium to larger organisations to be
   'Investors in People'.

There is an obvious role here for APEL, given that many of the
people currently in the workforce have enough experience and
knowledge to gain accreditation if only the facility were available
to them. Determination to reach or approach these targets will
highlight the possible use of APEL for these people, and will
present a relatively quick and cheap route for employers to work
towards achieving both national and local targets.

Output-related funding

Present funding of institutions offering further and higher education is calculated on the basis of target numbers of full-time
equivalent students. However, it is increasingly likely that in the
future at least part of the level of funding will be calculated
according to the 'output' of the institution. The precise definition
of 'output' is the cause of some discussion, but certainly one
element will be the achievement by learners of approved qualifications within the institution. This could, in theory, lead to a
cynical college choosing to market its provision at those members
of its community who are most likely to achieve high
resource-attracting qualifications. In some cases, these will be
NVQs. The more realistic approach will be to ensure that every
learner is given sufficient guidance to embark on a learning programme that is best suited to fit in with past experience and
future aspirations, at a pace and level that meet current needs.

There is a growing movement that seeks not only to define
outputs in terms of qualifications achieved, but also to encompass
less tangible evidence of progress, such as the educational 'distance
travelled' by a learner from the point of entry to the point of exit
from a learning programme. Demonstrated increased confidence
and self-awareness could become part of this definition of 'outcome', rather than 'output', and could thus provide an incentive for
reluctant institutions to look favourably on the use of APEL.

APEL provides a way in which the needs of the individual can be met through a process of reflection and action planning, in such a way that maximum distance is travelled in minimum time, by building on existing skills. At the same time, it can help to ensure that the institution targets provision where it is most needed, and where it is most likely to lead to successful and appropriate outcomes.

Record of Achievement

Within a very short period of time, all young people leaving school will do so with a Record of Achievement. This will be developed throughout their educational career and will detail not only school-based activities and academic success, but also any other interests and achievements that the individual, in consultation with teachers, wishes to include.

Such a record, which grows with a young person over many years, leaves adults at some disadvantage when it comes to progressing into education, training or employment. Developing an APEL portfolio allows adults to create their own record of achievement in a tangible form. Where the portfolio identifies skills which can be independently assessed and accredited, then adults are able to compete on equal footing with their younger counterparts in having demonstrably tradable assets in the education and employment markets.

Action planning

An inherent part of creating a record of achievement is developing an action plan relating to the next stage in an individual's learning progression route. A young person's action plan builds on the experiences and skills developed by the student in the recording of achievement during a period of attendance in school or college. The action plan itself is a statement of learning need as identified through this process. It thus facilitates decision-making, and provides the basis for negotiated action between the student and education and training providers.

An equivalent process for adults would be engaging in the APEL process. Thus a document, like that for a school-leaver, can be created that contains the following elements: statements of the knowledge, skills and experiences already acquired by the individual; educational, vocational or personal goals – preferably with a commitment to a realistic procedure and timetable for their achievement; any particular education or training needs; details of educational and training opportunities available to meet those needs.

Training credits

Training credits represent an entitlement to train to approved standards placed in the hands of young people leaving full-time education for the labour market. The credit enables them to 'buy' approved training from an employer or specialist provider. It is expected by the Government, and by the TECs and LECs who will administer the scheme, that holding the equivalent of a cash voucher for use for training will increase the motivation of young people to look for and come to expect continued training and education once they have left school.

This system can only work, however, if careers education and guidance are adequate, if they help the young person choose an appropriate course of action and 'spend' credits wisely. This will depend not only on the career aspirations of the individual, but also on the experiences being brought into the planning equation. Given that training credits are aimed at helping young people acquire NVQs, it may well be that, through APEL, even school-leavers will be able to claim units of competence already acquired, and make an appropriate and considered use of their credits that does not include receiving training for already acquired skills.

National Vocational Qualifications

A somewhat different notion of credits is incorporated within the NVQ framework. NVQs offer credit for demonstrated competence, in the form of a certificate of achievement. This credit, like training credits, can be held for later 'cashing in' – in this case against a whole NVQ rather than to buy training. Achieved units are transferable between awarding bodies issuing NVQ certificates in the same vocational area, and may also be transferable from one NVQ to another where identical units of competence occur in more than one qualification. Thus an information-processing unit assessed and certificated as part of a business adminstration qualification may also appear in, say, an information technology NVQ, and may be counted towards this should the learner later seek accreditation in this area.

The unit-based structure and the transferability of units from one area of competence to another makes the possibility of APEL a central feature of learner progression not only within a single vocational area, but across a range of areas.

An additional feature of NVQs is their definition of outcomes in terms of competence statements. These make the criteria for assessment and the desired competence completely overt, and so allow the possibility of gathering evidence of competence from a wide range of situations. This means that people re-entering training, education or work can use their experiences from home or other pursuits to demonstrate appropriate vocational skills. Their task is to relate their learning directly to the statements of competence as written in the NVQ, to provide evidence of their competence, and to seek assessment from an approved assessor. They can then receive certification of either one or more units, or a whole National Vocational Qualification.

In the context of NVQs, APL is seen as synonymous with assessment by portfolio against occupational standards. APEL seeks also to take into account the learning involved in creating such a portfolio.

Credit Accumulation and Transfer Schemes (CATS)

In addition to the 'banking' form of credit demonstrated by training credits and NVQs, the development of the notion of 'educational credit' is now becoming incorporated within both further and higher education. The credit involved in CAT schemes is recognition given to a learner on the basis of demonstrated learning outcomes related to a specified learning programme or qualification. A widespread CAT scheme operates within and between former polytechnics and other institutions of higher education.

The scheme is based on the principle that each programme of study within the institution is broken down into units, each of which is a self-contained section of study. Typically, a three-year degree course is deemed to be worth 360 credits – therefore one year of undergraduate study is worth 120 credits, usually made up of six units of 20 credit points each. Units, and therefore credits, are given a level that relates that unit to a first-, second- or third-year level of undergraduate study.

Credit can be awarded equally for study or for learning from experience, and so it can be added up not only across subject areas within the institution, but also across different types of learning. Skills and knowledge brought with the learner on entry can therefore be accredited. Sufficient accumulated credit can be used to claim a qualification.

Within this CAT scheme there is a difference between general and specific credit. General credit is calculated on the amount and quality of learning undertaken by a learner, regardless of context. Specific credit relates that learning to a particular programme of study. General credit may lead to exemption from a specified time within the programme of study (e.g. a term or a year). Specific credit may lead to exemption from particular parts of the course content (e.g. all the accounting units in the first year).

Such a credit-based system enhances the use of APEL and facilitates flexible and appropriate learning pathways for adult learners.

Open College Networks (OCNs)

Open College Networks are locally organised consortia of education and training providers. They also operate a credit system as a means of ascribing value to a set of learning outcomes. One credit is equal to the outcomes which could be achieved by an average learner in 30 hours' notional learning time, including taught, private and practical time. As within higher education CATS, these credits are awarded at different levels according to the complexity of learning involved, and the degree of autonomy demonstrated by the learner in achieving the specified outcomes. OCNs are authorised validating agencies for Access to Higher Education programmes, and so constitute a route into higher education for adults for whom the A Level route is not appropriate or attractive. This route also offers the possibility of the use of APEL in demonstrating learning at an appropriate level for standard entry into higher education.

The outcome-based nature of Open College Network recognised programmes also makes it possible for a learner to gain credit for prior learning by matching existing skills against a programme's outcomes and receiving the credits that are allocated to that programme.

OCN credits are awarded within a system of four levels, from basic skills and practical ability at Level 1 to autonomous study and the demonstration of analytical skills at Level 4. (See Appendix 2 for details of OCN processes.) Work is continuing to pilot methods whereby leavers may progress from OCN programmes towards NVQs.

National credit framework

There is currently intense interest and activity in the creation of a national credit framework for all post-16 qualifications. This would bring together all the existing initiatives and create open and accessible routes for learners across all the current, often artificial divides between vocational and academic qualifications, and adult, further and higher education. There can be no doubt that such a framework would greatly enhance the possibilities for the implementation of APEL.

As indicated above, there are currently two models of credit accumulation and transfer in operation in addition to the NVQ system of unit credit:

- HE CATS operating within and between institutions of higher education
- OCNs operating locally, but nationally co-ordinated by the National Open College Network, up to and including Access to Higher Education.

The Further Education Unit publication, *A Basis for Credit* (February 1992) outlines the issues that need to be addressed for the current systems to become united and expanded in order to create a framework that would also incorporate A Levels, AS Levels, GNVQs, GCSEs, and the proposed general and advanced diplomas. It seems likely that any such framework would use a model of notional time as a basis for a definition of credit. In such circumstances, it is very much easier to see how an individual can use a number and level of credits already achieved to gain access to further educational opportunities. APEL will be an integral constituent of such a framework.

Credits should not be confused with either units or modules. Units are essentially to do with outcomes associated with a part of a qualification or programme of study. Modules are linked to the content and delivery of a part of a qualification or programme. Credits represent a way of ascribing value to identified learning however and wherever this has taken place. Credit is, therefore, the 'currency' of an educational system which measures achievement and ensures consistency across all agencies participating in a transfer agreement.

Even within the current use of the two CAT models and NVQs, it is possible to see how credit transfer could operate across the frameworks. OCNs already have established links into the HE admissions process through their status as Authorised Validating Agencies. An agreed number of credits at OCN Level 4 grants the learner standard entry into higher education.

Processes are close to being established whereby NVQ awarding bodies will recognise NVQ units assessed within the context of an OCN programme, thus facilitating progression from local access points into a national qualification framework. The further development of NVQ Levels 4 and 5 will lead to an inevitable link between assessment at this level and other provision within institutions of higher education. All of these developments broaden the likelihood of the increased use of APEL in the future.

The above description of existing credit accumulation and transfer systems is not in any way to deny the existence and valuable contribution of the Open University system of credit accumulation within its degree structure. However, in terms of its inherently internal nature, the Open University credit system is not currently seen as part of the wider national developments on credit accumulation and transfer. The Open University does, however, operate a system of APEL, where the prior learning and achievement of potential students is taken into account and may lead to credit or advanced standing towards an award.

General National Vocational Qualifications (GNVQs)

Although still at the piloting stage, GNVQs are set to have a dramatic impact on the face of post-16 education. They are designed to maintain the characteristics of NVQs, i.e:

- specified in the form of outcomes
- made up of a number of units
- allow credit for each unit separately
- allow credit accumulation for the award of a whole GNVQ
- award credit for those who meet the required standard, irrespective of time, place or method of learning
- allow open access to assessment with a range of evidence acceptable

- be subject to the same quality assurance procedures as NVQs.

However, where GNVQs are distinct from NVQs is that they seek to assess the skills, knowledge and understanding that underpin a range of NVQs, and do not assess occupational or professional competence in any of the specific areas of work covered by NVQs. They will 'prepare people either to go on to more demanding job-specific training or to higher education. GNVQs will test the kinds of skill which can be used in a whole range of occupations – such as communication, problem-solving, information technology and language skills' (Michael Portillo, Employment Secretary, 1992).

It is clear from this that not only will GNVQs lend themselves to APEL by virtue of their structure, but because of their interest in broader issues than occupationally specific competence, may prove particularly attractive to adults who are seeking a formative assessment leading to further development. APEL may provide a particularly apposite means of achieving this.

Flexible delivery systems

The current desire to meet the varied training and educational needs of all sectors of our society, to increase access to lifelong education and training for all, and to respond to the commercial realities of Britain as we move towards the next century, has led colleges to review their traditional roles and the way in which they fulfil them. The result has been a move away from course-based to learner-centred provision, where learners are more able to have a personally designed programme of study.

In order to meet the needs of individuals, the face of colleges is changing. They are increasingly incorporating a range of flexibly delivered learning and assessment opportunities. These include modularisation of the curriculum, workshop-based delivery, 'assessment on demand', open and distance learning. Exponents of APEL like to claim that APEL has been the driving force behind such developments, on the basis that if the educational rationale behind APEL is accepted, then the rest cannot fail to follow. It is, after all, impossible to give credit if there is no credit framework in place. It is impossible to offer and implement a realistic personalised action plan without the facility to offer guidance and the opportunity to work towards specific goals. Access to assessment on demand can most easily be achieved through a modular curriculum structure and open workshops.

APEL AS PART OF THE AGENDA FOR ADULT LEARNERS

APEL is primarily, though not exclusively, of importance and relevance to adult learners. As such, it will only be possible to address its implementation fully as part of a whole agenda geared to the needs of adult learners within colleges. Adults are essentially different from their younger counterparts in college, chiefly because, unlike the younger people, they are not preparing for independent life – they are in the midst of living it. Colleges have the challenge of making their provision for adults, as well as for young people, a process of liberation, enabling them to recognise and make use of their skills, talents and abilities, and to make choices about the world in which they live.

If we compare the proportion of time spent in the education system with the breadth and timespan of human development, it becomes obvious that more learning takes place outside educational institutions than within them. Learning is a part of life itself. Yet there is an ethos that has grown over the years that implies that the only valuable learning is that which takes place in a teaching institution. This concept is now being widely challenged – by employers who, under the auspices and influence of TECs, are increasingly undertaking training and assessment for and with their staff; by NCVQ through the creation of competence-based qualifications; by awarding bodies through not only the award of NVQs, but also other competence-based qualifications such as the RSA Advanced Diploma in the Organisation of Community Groups; and by colleges who are moving their role away from that of teaching institutions mainly for young people aged 16 to 19, to undertake work-based assessment and customised learning programmes for employers and employees.

Adult education has always been the most vulnerable sector of the education system, and the latest Further and Higher Education Act has served to highlight this fact yet again. After incorporation, the LEA will continue to fund non-vocational provision, while the Further Education Funding Council (FEFC) will fund provision falling into 'Schedule 2' – mainly vocational courses and access routes into them. Where community or adult education embraces both elements, it becomes vulnerable as priorities for funding may lead to compartmentalising provision and limiting easy access to progression. The response of colleges will be crucial to the future of adult education as they will have it in their power to create and foster links between what is currently defined as non-vocational or leisure and other programmes of study.

The diverse nature of adult learners with their different reasons for studying poses a challenge for colleges and other educational and training institutions. Adults do not return to education without due thought and consideration. Unlike many young learners, they are not in college to defer a decision about future careers, or because it is what is expected of them by family and friends. They come to college for a whole host of reasons:

- because they want to learn
- because they feel they have things to finish that they did not finish at school
- because they were not yet ready to take up the challenge of learning during their school careers
- because of a major life change – marriage or divorce, a birth or a death in the family, children going to school, children leaving home, a new job, redundancy.

They are, therefore, not in college by either coincidence or compulsion; and part of the reason for being there at all is that they have begun to identify their learning needs. The college therefore has an obligation to pick up on this motivation and use it as the starting point for building something that can meet the needs of the learner.

However, life is not made easy for adults wishing to have their prior learning recognised or to undertake further learning within a taught context. They are beset by barriers erected by a variety of circumstances. They encounter personal problems arising from domestic responsibilities and relationships, and need, often, to renegotiate roles and duties. They may suffer guilt at causing disruption to the lives of others for what is often seen as the selfishness of their desire to study. Many have difficulty adapting to the role of student after having taken a leading or teaching function in their home and work lives.

There are almost always financial problems connected with returning to college arising from reduced earnings. These are compounded by a grants and benefits system that is designed with young, full-time learners in mind, and which discriminates against the adult learner wishing to adopt a part-time route to study, or threatens to reduce benefits on return to full-time study. Most colleges are managing to find ways around some of these problems, but the pressure is still exerted on the learner, who has feelings of 'I shouldn't be here' reinforced by the system.

Adult learners are also faced with academic and institutional problems. How to sort out the maze of options available, and where they all lead. How to get a timetable that fits in with personal needs. How to ensure that childcare is available during the times a chosen programme runs. How to make sure that children are collected from school should the timetable run across school hours. There are social issues that arise for a mature student in a predominantly 16- to 19-year-old environment, where the issues of age, interests, domestic commitments and relationships are not always taken into account, and where the material used in teaching is geared to the needs and experience of younger learners. The practice of 'infilling' adult learners on to full-time courses therefore often proves inappropriate and leads to more dissatisfaction than a parallel programme designed specifically for adults.

A college committed to equality of opportunity through a flexible and learner-centred structure, including APEL, can begin to address many of these problems faced by adult learners. The most valuable resource invested into college is not money, but learner time. This is particularly true, for all the reasons outlined above, in the case of adult learners. It is therefore incumbent on the college not to waste that most valuable resource.

Experience seems to point to the fact that a system that addresses all these issues because of a desire to meet the needs of adult learners, also provides a better learning environment for all its learners. There are, however, very real organisational problems for colleges that wish to meet the needs of adult learners and to implement APEL as part of the process. The increasing emphasis on output-related funding makes APEL theoretically simple and logical, but presently most colleges are essentially course based, with flexible learning opportunities being the exception rather than the rule. The result of this kind of structure is that staff are fully timetabled into classroom delivery, and it requires a new flexibility of thought as well as college structure to release them to undertake other duties.

Even under a system of output-related funding, income may only be sustained if there is increased participation. APEL may provide this increase in learner participation through attracting a new sector of the community. It may also increase 'output' in terms of qualifications or part qualifications, and provide student satisfaction more appropriately than many other systems, if sufficient investment is made in it at the outset.

All the experience gained so far in attempting to implement APEL points to two very clear messages:

- Leadership and support from senior management is essential.
- If external pump-priming moneys are used, there needs to be a clear strategic plan as to how the work will continue once the external funding has stopped.

These both arise from the fact that APEL cannot easily be a short-term, 'bolt-on' provision.

It may be that the college intends to implement APEL within a separate full-cost unit. However, there is still the need, in some way, to provide facilities for guidance and 'topping up' as well as assessment and accreditation. Such facilities will probably be available within the college, but learner access to them must be accounted for in staff and resource allocation. Often external funding has been used to release staff for development work. However, this is by definition a short-term arrangement. The results must be embedded within college provision if expectations among staff and potential learners are not to be raised and dashed. It is unrealistic to expect middle managers and their teams to invest time and effort in reorganising programmes, staffing and timetables without overt support and commitment from the very top of the management structure.

The general lesson that has been learned by colleges that have begun to implement APEL is that they need to be realistic about what they can achieve, and must introduce change step by step rather than by wholesale restructuring. The introduction of APEL requires a fundamental restructuring of sections of the institutions, and therefore requires a clear, phased action plan for implementation. Such a plan needs to set long- and short-term objectives within a set timescale, taking into account the staffing and resourcing needs, staff and organisational development needs, and the likelihood of some staff resistance to change.

Whether, in this range of contexts, APEL is the cart or the horse in terms of leading or following institutional development, there can be no doubt that it fits neatly into an institution where flexibility and individual learning are central organisational themes, and are underpinned by a policy of equality of opportunity and maximum benefit to the learner, implemented through a strong guidance base and a range of learning and assessment opportunities.

Chapter 2

How does APEL work?

INTRODUCTION

The fundamental processes of any APEL, whether specifically intended to seek NVQ accreditation or some other outcome, are based on seven key stages for the learner:

- initial counselling
- recognising and identifying skills
- relating these skills to an agreed set of outcomes or criteria
- gathering evidence of these skills
- documentation of evidence
- assessment of the evidence
- accreditation.

If APEL is to be a part of a range of college provision, it is essential that it is seen as, at the very least, part of a process of initial assessment. As such, it can never be dissociated from a strong guidance base. It will therefore be necessary for each APEL candidate to be assigned a counsellor or support worker who is conversant not only with the principles and practices of APEL, but also with the principles and practices of good educational guidance. These centre on a service that is client centred, confidential, impartial and accessible, and which seeks to inform, advise, counsel, assess, enable, advocate and give feedback. In this way, guidance can be seen to take its own distinctive place in the triangle of guidance, provision and assessment that leads both individuals and institutions to a clearer picture of what is being provided and where it could lead.

One of the distinctive features of APEL is that it is designed around the individual learner. No two people have the same experiences, so no two people will present the same profile of learning. Certainly many people will arrive at similar action plans, but the reasons for creating them and the processes of arriving at a definition of needs will be totally individual. An APEL service must, therefore, by definition be client centred: if it is not, it is not APEL.

In order to believe in the process, the candidate must be able to trust in the counsellor not to divulge any confidential information that is disclosed during the process of reflection that is the starting point of the APEL process. Receipt of such information must be accepted by the counsellor on trust. It follows from this that the counsellor must be impartial and non-judgemental about any information shared.

The counsellor should also be prepared to allow the learner to decide on what is an appropriate progression route, however unorthodox this may seem in the light of usual combinations of learning programmes. The recognition of existing skills and aptitudes may lead individuals into a range of further learning opportunities that appear to have little coherence. Although the relative benefits of following a more traditional pattern may be pointed out, the choice should ultimately lie with the learner, not the counsellor.

Given the many constraints – financial, social, psychological and temporal – under which adult learners are often operating, an initial guidance service for adult learners should also, ideally, be free of charge and easily accessible.

The APEL process places demands and obligations on all participants in its operation – the learner, the counsellor and the host institution. As this section of the book addresses and describes each stage of the process, it will also signal some of the roles and responsibilities of those involved.

Figure 1 demonstrates how APEL can be seen in terms of a progression cycle, from the learner's point of view.

The college that seeks to help learners address these questions, and to establish appropriate ways forward, will need to create pathways that support the learner through the APEL process, which is indicated in Figure 2.

The relative emphasis placed on each of the stages in Figure 2 will vary depending on the starting position of each individual learner. The use of APEL in adult or community education contexts tends to concentrate primarily on the first two or three

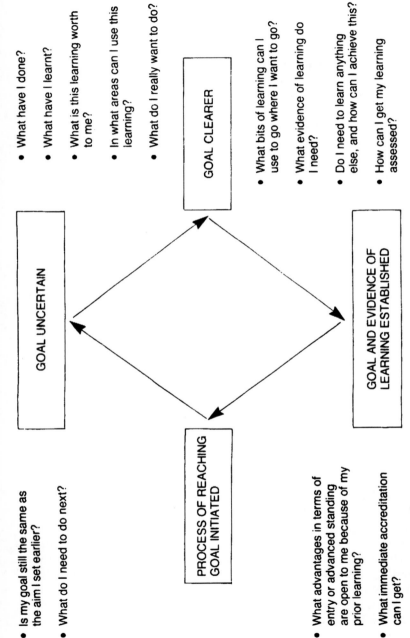

- What have I done?
- What have I learnt?
- What is this learning worth to me?
- In what areas can I use this learning?
- What do I really want to do?

GOAL CLEARER

- What bits of learning can I use to go where I want to go?
- What evidence of learning do I need?
- Do I need to learn anything else, and how can I achieve this?
- How can I get my learning assessed?

GOAL UNCERTAIN

GOAL AND EVIDENCE OF LEARNING ESTABLISHED

PROCESS OF REACHING GOAL INITIATED

- Is my goal still the same as the aim I set earlier?
- What do I need to do next?

- What advantages in terms of entry or advanced standing are open to me because of my prior learning?
- What immediate accreditation can I get?

Figure 1 Cycle of learner progression

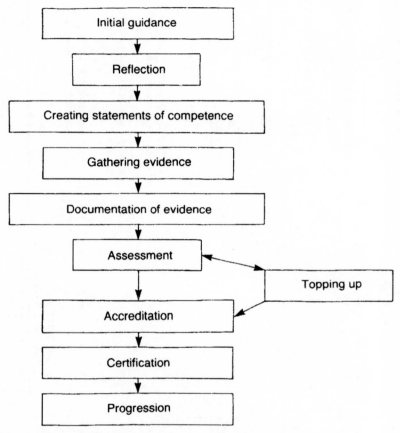

Figure 2 The APEL process

stages. This is because the clientele with whom tutors are working and for whom APEL may be seen to be appropriate are often those people who would find direct entry into mainstream education, training or work very difficult. They have often had negative experiences at school, which have left them feeling 'unqualified failures', and the local, supportive atmosphere of the adult education centre can help them build and increase confidence.

Typically, the first stages of the process have been found to be extremely effective in parent and toddler groups, women's groups, job search activities, assertiveness training, and with individuals with disabilities or other special needs. Work has also been done with refugees and ethnic minority groups, where it is possible to recognise and value skills gained in another cultural context and assess their relevance and applicability in Britain. Pilot work is being undertaken in prisons and the probation service to assess the scope of APEL for offenders and ex-offenders.

APEL in a work or vocational training setting may concentrate more on the latter stages of the process, as the need is to find rapid and appropriate progression for people who already have some recognised competence but need to match this to an appropriate framework to facilitate progress. The process may therefore be used to match skills to a job description or to part or all of a qualification.

The success of APEL in this range of contexts lies in the fact that one of the first issues to be addressed in the planning of a progression route is the identification of the point from which a learner is starting. APEL, with its intrinsically individual approach, allows time and support in reaching such a state of con- sciousness. For some individuals, it will be enough simply to acknowledge and believe in the skills that are revealed in the reflection process. Others will want to take the whole exercise further and seek accreditation within an appropriate framework.

INITIAL GUIDANCE

Bearing in mind that APEL is not the appropriate route for every adult learner, the availability of initial counselling and guidance is crucial. Some learners approaching a training or educational institution will have a clear picture of what they want, and a vision of how they can get there. They are unlikely, given the novelty of APEL and its restricted usage, to know that this route exists, or its applicability to them. It is at the initial counselling stage that the possibility is raised, and all the implications of choosing APEL are pointed out to the learner:

- the time-saving aspects
- the flexibility
- the valuing of non-work-based experience
- the range of areas in which APEL is offered
- the time involved in evidence gathering

- the potentially solitary process
- the support that will be available
- the range of attendance patterns for 'topping up' or acquiring new skills.

As a result of this counselling process, some learners will choose APEL. Others will reject it out of hand as they want all the benefits of attending a learning programme, and need to learn new skills rather than have previous ones recognised.

Others will not immediately see the relevance of seeking accreditation for their prior learning, as they are not convinced they have any skills to accredit. It is this group who may well benefit from spending some time, either individually or in the company of other people, exploring where their skills, abilities and aptitudes lie. This will take them on to the next phase of the APEL process.

A typical example of this is the woman who worked in an office before having her children and who now assumes that office work is the only option open to her. This is, in her eyes, the only 'real' experience that she has. She sees her needs as being the updating of previously acquired skills, in order to get back into familiar work as quickly as possible. What she may not admit is that she never really liked the work first time round, and she may have no idea of how different the modern office is from the one she worked in. After counselling, it may well transpire that an office skills course is precisely what she wants, and the possibility of using APEL to speed up the process of gaining updated qualifications can be explored with a specialist counsellor or tutor in this area. However, on the basis of the many sides of her personality that she has discovered and developed during her years working at home caring for her family, she may equally reveal a yen to train as a nursery nurse, counsellor, supervisor, manager or caterer, or even simply to 'compete' with her partner or children by studying for a degree. APEL may be equally relevant in pursuing any of these ends, and may be explored at this stage.

Investment in this first counselling stage is a prerequisite for the access of learners to APEL either for direct accreditation or as a means of exploring other progression routes.

Roles and responsibilities in initial counselling

The learner will:

- decide upon the appropriateness or otherwise of following the APEL route, either with the aim of seeking an accelerated route to accreditation, or in order to explore unrecognised skills for the purposes of defining a progression route.

The counsellor will:

- help the learner identify specific needs
- give information on the range of options available, and advise on their appropriateness to the needs of the particular learner.

The institution will:

- recognise the value of initial guidance
- commit time and resources to training staff to acquire the necessary counselling skills
- allow time and space for the counselling process to take place
- provide a range of support facilities such as:
  - ◆ course and institution prospectuses
  - ◆ checklists of learning outcomes of programmes on offer
  - ◆ expert systems and other self-assessment materials for use by learners
  - ◆ bilingual counsellors
  - ◆ creche
  - ◆ wheelchair access to the institution.

Case study 2.1

Catering studies

The intake for City and Guild 706.1 in a college was 80 students. The 706.1 (Basic Catering), the first year of a two-year course, was already fully modularised. 706.2 (Cookery for the Catering Industry), to which successful students would progress for their second year, was partially modularised. The students were mainly mature people, many in employment. Many of those who were employed worked for the council as, for example, school meal providers.

The students were individually interviewed by a member of the catering teaching staff, and, where appropriate, given the option of being accredited and given exemption from the first year of the course immediately, or, if they preferred, to join the class prior to assessment and then take the exemption option. Twenty students were found to be eligible for accreditation and exemption from part of the course. Eight students were seen as eligible for accreditation and exemption from the whole of 706.1.

The response of the students was unexpected. All declined the offer of advanced standing. Those in employment saw it as a positive advantage to be away from work for one day a week for two years instead of one, especially as the first year was going to be very easy for them. They already had agreement from their employers that the fees would be paid, and could see no reason to change the arrangements that had been made. They were not seeking promotion, and so gathering qualifications quickly was not a priority. They were also attending college with colleagues from work, and were reluctant to be made to seem 'different' by moving faster than their friends. They were reluctant to be moved into a second-year group where they knew no one. Even those who were self-financing seemed to have made the psychological commitment to two years' attendance and were unwilling to change their minds.

In the event, all the students eligible for advanced standing, accreditation or exemption chose to stay with the whole two-year course, which raised a whole number of issues with regard to the APEL procedure.

Conclusions

The in-depth counselling of the students took place in September, when they had already enrolled for the course. The option of a 'fast route' had not beeen mentioned to them or their employers before then, and so came as a surprise. On reflection, it would have been helpful if the initial counselling process had been carried out in June or July, so that initial assessment could have placed the students into the 'right' course immediately, instead of leaving it until they thought they were about to start their two-year course. This would also have been at a time when tutors were under less pressure, with time to undertake assessment. It would also have left time for further recruitment where students could have been referred straight to the second-year programme.

At that time, the admissions unit was in the initial stages of development. Now it is completed, all students will be interviewed there first, rather than being referred straight to the catering department. The general principles of APEL can then be presented to the students without their feeling pressurised by a tutor who is going to be teaching them later on. It will also avoid the problem of group 'bonding' which had already taken place in this group by the time the APEL option was offered, so that there was understandable reluctance to leave the group that was intended to be the peer group, and enter another ready-formed group.

It was also decided by all the staff involved that more work needed to be done to inform employers of the existence of APEL. Moreover, it was important to emphasise the reduced costs that would accrue to them by their employees gaining qualifications in a reduced timescale, and the advantages of students being helped to identify their own strengths and abilities, rather than attending a course that would, in some cases, teach them what they already knew.

RECOGNISING AND IDENTIFYING SKILLS

For many adults, one of the hardest things to do is to say what they are good at, especially if this is not set in a specific vocational context.

People who are employed, and have confidence in their ability to do their job, may find it relatively easy to talk about their skills in a specific work context. Indeed, some are so good at doing this that they are promoted above what their colleagues consider to be their capability. For instance, a computer programmer may be able to wax most lyrical on the ins and outs of programs, hardware, the relative merits of one package against another. But could the same person give a confident account of her ability to participate in a neighbourhood watch meeting? Is the superb works manager able to claim equal managerial competence in the home? Could the harassed parent precisely quantify the many and varied skills that are involved in pacifying squabbling children, making sure that the household routines meet the needs of all members, ensuring a supply of food or clean laundry?

It is all too easy to underestimate, or even ignore, the wide range of skills that we all acquire as we take on increased autonomy and responsibility, whether this is at work, at home, or in leisure activities. In order for any claims of competence to be made through APEL, skills need to be identified, and this may often involve the process of linking skills acquired in one context to those required in another. In order to achieve this, it is necessary to enter into an often lengthy period of reflection. Parallels between work and home life are often not obvious, and many people seeking to move into new areas of work assume that they are doing so with a blank sheet of experience in the new sphere. After a period of supported reflection, they are usually able to identify the particular learning that will assist their entry into their chosen new direction, and which may give them a substantial start on their way.

This stage of the APEL process is for many people the time when they suddenly realise that the 'only' label that they thought they had to wear ('only a housewife', 'only a redundant steel worker') is, in fact, a mirage. The process of sitting down, with a supportive tutor, mentor, friend or partner, can lead to revelations about areas of unnoticed aptitudes, interests and abilities. The process has to be carefully handled, as any such exercise is almost bound to take learners back into areas of their past life that have been problematic or difficult. However, for most people who lack the confidence to state at the outset where their abilities lie, and claim them against a set of vocational or academic criteria, it is important to review large areas of the past in order to identify the points at which learning occurred, what form that learning took, and how it can be re-presented to be of value in a future planning process.

It is important to remember here that past experiences are being recalled in order to identify not the events themselves, but the learning that can be identified as having arisen from that experience. APEL is not a means of accrediting life, but a means of accrediting learning. It may be, for example, that a bereavement, identified as a key point in a learner's past, could lead to learning about counselling skills, independent living, dealing with benefits systems, buying and selling houses, the workings of probate and the legal system, etc. The bereavement is the event that enables the learner to develop and later identify the skills and knowledge acquired at that time.

In this generalised form, there is not a lot of competence that can be claimed for the purposes of accreditation. However, with a little discussion, some careers input and some course or qualification outcomes to refer to, it may be possible for an individual to use the learning towards a career move or a training course. Immediate possibilities that spring to mind are the caring professions, benefits officer, lawyer or legal executive. The key to this part of the process is trying to identify transferable skills; not simply asking 'What am I good at?', but following this up with 'Where could I use this skill?'

Let us look at an example of how this might work. A further education lecturer feels in need of a career move. Because there is no appraisal system in place in her college, she has no clear picture of where her skills lie, or what she should be planning to improve on for future years. However, she feels she generates a good rapport with her students, manages to keep full classes every year, and spends a lot of time counselling her students both during the course and when they come to leave college. She therefore feels that she offers a good service to her students from the start to the finish of their contact with her and the college. But she is dissatisfied with being in the same place all the time, and would like to find a job that can take her out and about a bit more, meeting different people rather than the fairly similar student groups that she teaches every year.

She starts to take the local paper and look at jobs on a fairly regular basis. Most of them are not suitable because of pay, or they offer nothing that her present job does not already offer. The only expanding market seems to be in selling. This is not a career she had ever envisaged being interested in, but it meets many of her desired criteria for job satisfaction – travelling, a sense of uncertainty and excitement, non-routine, working with people, reasonable money, with the sky the limit if you get good at it. But she has never sold anything in her life, so how could she possibly think about this area of work? However, with a bit of encouragement from her friends, she decides to apply for a selling job.

Her successful application rests on trying to convince her future employer that she has the skills to do the job, even if she has no immediately identifiable track record in the work. She thinks about what the job of selling would involve, and compares it with her role as lecturer.

- She has a product to sell – her course.
- She identifies a market – her potential students among school-leavers.
- She targets publicity at that market – direct visits to schools, publicity materials, liaison with careers and teaching staff, individual interview with potential students.
- She packages the product – timetable, college facilities, course content and delivery.
- She delivers within an agreed timescale – the course is completed before the time of the examination/assessment.
- She allows for personal preference – self-directed work through projects and personal case studies.
- She tests customer satisfaction – tutorial work, exam results and course end evaluation.
- She gives advice on a range of alternative products on offer – guidance concerning other courses, further training and careers advice.

Once she has analysed her present skills and abilities by placing them in the context of her planned next job, it is relatively easy to write a letter of application that presents these skills convincingly to a future employer in the field of selling. An imaginative employer will be impressed by anyone who can present a well-argued case. The success or failure in terms of gaining the job will rest on the interview skills of the candidate, and the genuine enthusiasm for the work that she shows.

This example shows how reflection in order to identify past experience and skills can work in order to assist in career moves. The process is also of extreme value for people who are presently outside the paid-work environment, but have skills that could well be used within paid labour. There are very few jobs that are being done for money in our society that are not being done by someone else in an unpaid or voluntary capacity. It is not hard to create a lengthy list to illustrate this point – childminding, domestic management, caring, car driver, home improvement, committee chair, animal minder, advice worker, artist, etc. The problem lies in moving from one context to another, and this can only be done by identifying and relating those skills acquired in the one situation to those necessary for entry into another.

The end of this phase should result in the learner being able to make statements relating to areas of competence, whether these be related to a specific vocational field ('I can measure a room and estimate the amount of wallpaper needed to redecorate') or more general 'core skills' statements ('I can relate sympathetically to elderly people'). These statements then become the building blocks upon which the rest of the APEL process will develop.

The amount of time needed during this phase will vary from learner to learner. Someone with a fairly clear set of possible objectives, and building on known work-related competence, may simply be able to identify and write them down in a format suitable for initial assessment. Other people, especially those whose self-confidence is low, may need a longer period of reflection as they come not only to recognise the existence of skills, but also to believe in them. It may be necessary for the APEL counsellor to call upon the services of other professionals within and beyond the education field in helping the learner to build up a positive self-image and create a clearer picture of where current and potential skills and aptitudes may lead.

Roles and responsibilities in recognising and identifying skills

The learner will:

- engage in APEL initially through a process of reflection
- use this period of reflection to consolidate first thoughts about using APEL towards a qualification or career move
- create a list of competences or skills that demonstrate a range of general and occupationally specific abilities.

The counsellor will:

- support the learner through providing 'prompting' exercises to stimulate and encourage focused reflection
- help the learner formulate statements of achievements and abilities
- enable the learner to create a positive self-image

- liaise with other agencies on behalf of the learner where further advice and support is needed.

The institution will:

- ensure the availability of appropriately qualified counselling staff
- allocate tutor time and appropriate accommodation for learner support
- ensure the availability of, for example, careers advisers to support the role of the APEL counsellor.

Case study 2.2

Communications – a text-driven approach for adult basic education students

Whilst it was recognised by a tertiary college that individual vocational areas would feel the impact of APEL and would be able to implement it through a modularised curriculum, it was felt that the greatest degree of cross-programme understanding of the process could be achieved through concentrating some effort on accrediting prior learning of communications skills. Staff undertook to write new teaching materials and evolve a new curriculum structure for this area, which would guide the provision of all adult basic education and provide key open learning resources. It would also be a major feature of the core communications needs being identified in most programme areas of the college, and serve as the basis of communications skills as part of core skills across the college and as part of GNVQs.

The whole programme structure consists of six modules which concentrate on developing understanding of written texts through certain 'focus skills', key concepts, a wide-ranging common content, and both reflective and externally moderated evaluation techniques. The modules include texts that explore environmental issues, the black diaspora, the Anne Frank diaries and the creative writing of a range of basic education students from a variety of ethnic backgrounds. The programme is accredited through the local Open College Federation at Levels 2 and 3.

The introductory module (known as the IPEL module – Identifying Prior and Experiential Learning) consists of five key texts to support the process of identifying communication skills. The first text is general, and the others cover schooling, parenting, work and hobbies. Using the model texts, constructing life/time lines and examining their own life material, students proceed to identify major life events, and the skills and experiences active in these events. These are then 'translated' into statements of personal competence. Learners then go on to identify possible progression routes into training and/or employment.

From working through the texts, students demonstrate competence in core communication skills, comprehension, extended reading and listening, and extended writing. At the end of the module, they have identified their prior learning, in terms of both taught and certificated learning and experiential learning, and have arrived at a positive self-description on their own terms. This programme now forms the basis of all basic education work within the college.

Conclusions

1 There has been a marked increase in confidence shown by students participating in the IPEL module and a similar rise in tutor expectation of students.
2 The availability of the provison through the open learning workshop means that tutors can easily refer students and potential students to the programme. The flexibility given by open learning also means that the much-needed support in preparing a portfolio identifying and giving evidence of communication skills can also be given more or less on demand.
3 The programme has been recognised as valuable by all the major vocational areas within the college, and has helped raise the profile and credibility of APEL across the college.

RELATING SKILLS TO CRITERIA

If the identified learning is to be used towards a further learning outcome, it needs to be set in a context. Probably the easiest way to demonstrate this is to use some of the national standards for NVQs, which are conveniently divided into units and elements and which thus provide a ready framework. For the sake of simplicity, let us look at the area of Business Administration.

In order to gain a Level 1 NVQ in Business Administration, an individual needs to demonstrate competence in nine units. One of these is a unit entitled 'Filing'. In accordance with the pattern of all NVQs, the Filing unit is divided into elements; in this case, two:

- file documents and open new files within an established filing system
- identify and retrieve documents from within an established filing system.

Each element is accompanied by a set of performance criteria that define the competence in more detail. Thus the performance criteria for the first element are:

- All documents filed without undue delay in correct location and sequence.
- All materials stored without damage in a safe and secure manner.
- All documents correctly classified.
- Classification uncertainties referred to an appropriate authority.

In order for a complete element or unit to be awarded, all the performance criteria must be seen to be met. The smallest part of an NVQ that can be certificated is a unit, but each element is separately documented on completion. An NVQ can, therefore, be acquired over a period of time, in accordance with the learner's current ability and learning needs.

In addition to the performance criteria, each element carries with it a range statement, which indicates the range of circumstances under which competence must be demonstrated. Still referring to the first element of the Filing unit, the Range Statement reads as follows:

> The Competence includes paper-based filing systems covering the storage and retrieval of information using alphabetical and numerical filing and indexing systems and lateral and vertical filing methods. It requires competence in pre-sorting documents for filing, setting up, sorting and sequencing card

indexes and cross-reference material for filing, and preparing and introducing new files.

Additionally, the element stipulates the underpinning knowledge and skills that must be demonstrated before the learner can be considered competent. These are:

- importance of effective storage of information
- classifying documents
- organisational filing systems and procedures including special and confidential files and retention policy
- characteristics of effective classification and filing systems
- filing and indexing systems (e.g. alphabetical, numerical)
- filing methods (e.g. lateral, vertical)
- planning and organising work within deadlines
- dexterity in sorting, handling and storing documents.

(Performance standards for administrative business and commercial staff – Administrative Business and Commercial Training Group)

Any learners who have worked in an office environment, whether in a paid or unpaid capacity, will be familiar with the concept of filing. They are likely to know why a filing system is necessary, where to find documents, how to operate the system in place in their particular office, and who should have access to what information. They may also know about and be able to describe the operation of filing systems that are different from the one they use. It would thus be relatively easy for them to demonstrate that they have the necessary knowledge and skills to begin to claim competence in this element.

The basis of NVQs is that they relate to vocational competence, and assessment should therefore ideally be carried out in the workplace, or through a simulation that as closely as possible matches a real working environment. However, for the purposes of APEL, the learner is asked to provide evidence that proves to the assessor that competence has been gained that equates to that of a learner in a workplace. In order for this to become a reality, it is essential that the learner has a full picture of exactly what the stipulated statements of competence are, so that appropriate evidence can be gathered to prove personal competence. Again, for people with a work background to call on, this may not prove too arduous a task.

However, learners who are returning to college or training with either no paid work experience or work experience in a different vocational context may fail to recognise the relevance of their experience in terms of a qualification. They will therefore need help in selecting from their prior learning and experience those parts that can be shown to have vocational relevance in a given context. In order to be able to do this, they will need a clear picture not only of their own skills, but also of the range of contexts in which they may be of use to them.

If we return to the NVQ Businesss Administration qualification, and its Filing unit, it can be seen how the system can operate. Most households have some sort of rudimentary filing system for bills, school reports, recipes, household documents, etc. In terms of APEL, this could be the basis of evidence of competence in the Filing unit. The learner needs to be given the full criteria for achievement of each element of the unit, and collect evidence of having met all the criteria. The existence of the learning relating to filing, where and how this learning has been acquired, will have been revealed by the previous stages of reflection and the creation of statements of competence. Matching the learning to the framework of the NVQ may lead to accreditation, and give the learner a boost up the qualifications ladder, while at the same time building the confidence to continue up that ladder.

The NVQ framework makes APEL relatively simple to apply. However, this is not the only qualification framework within which APEL can be applied. Any programme of learning or award that is defined in terms of outcomes rather than content is, in theory, accessible through APEL. Many courses offered by the major national awarding bodies and those offered by other education and training institutions are now presented in outcome form. Many are broken down into units or modules, and the learning required for successful completion identified in terms of 'can do' statements. There has thus been a move away from the syllabus-based, norm-referenced assessment process (as still exists in A Levels) to a system that makes explicit to the learner at the outset the outcomes and assessment criteria for the programme and its constituent parts. The basis of this formula is that evidence of achievement is being sought in all the stated outcomes, and this will demonstrate competence in the programme/unit/module. It therefore becomes feasible for a great many qualifications or parts of qualifications to be gained through APEL, in a range of education and training settings.

In order to help learners identify appropriate frameworks within which to place their identified skills, they will need substantial information about possible progression routes, starting points, entry requirements and intended learning outcomes. In the college context, this can be initiated by the creation of a series of checklists relating to courses or qualifications on offer, that give clear outline criteria of what is expected of the learner. Many adult learners are unable to meet entry requirements that are defined in terms of academic attainment (e.g. five GCSEs) and the catch-all 'or equivalent' is often inadequate for those people who are unsure of, or underestimate, their own capabilities or potential.

Where learners are looking to enter a programme of study, it will be helpful for them to be given a statement along the lines of 'In order to derive maximum benefit from this programme, you should have the following skills before you join.' The checklist could then detail required levels of literacy, numeracy or other core skills, as well as any specific or specialist knowledge needed (e.g. working with scale drawings, competence in double-entry book-keeping, basic knowledge of conversational French).

A parallel checklist can also be provided that details the areas that will be assessed during the programme, the form and criteria of the assessment, and what the learner should be able to do on successfully completing all assessment requirements. This summative checklist will state: 'In order to be awarded this qualification, you will have to have been assessed to standard on the following skills and knowledge.' If this is further broken down into the outcomes of each unit or module, then the creation and implementation of personal action plans, and exemption from part or all of the qualification through APEL, become a much easier process.

The creation of such checklists has a range of benefits:

- It gives the learner a clear framework within which to assess current competence and plan future action within a cycle of learning.
- It gives the guidance worker or counsellor a set of information to use with individual learners.
- It helps tutors to focus on the central issues of learning programmes and the desired outcomes of qualifications.
- It gives the institution an audit of current learning programmes and enables overlap of provision to be identified and used in strategic planning.

However, for a learner choosing to continue through APEL, the following stages of the process are hard, and the benefits must be weighed up against the effort to be invested. A rough rule of thumb might be that if a learner can readily see where evidence can be gathered to prove competence in 50 per cent of the checklist items (whether this is at unit or module level, or across a whole qualification), then it is probably worth the effort of choosing the APEL route rather than attending a course of study. Any less than 50 per cent, and the amount of top-up learning that will have to be undertaken will make the process more arduous than attending the programme.

These rough calculations will, of course, need to be set within the context of the learner's own circumstances. A learner who has great difficulty getting to college may still choose to work through the APEL process, and identify ways in which evidence can be gathered or generated to fulfil the criteria at present missing from the list of acquired skills. The counsellor will need to take all such issues into account when working with learners and be prepared to think laterally on ways and means to generate evidence.

Employers wishing to use APEL for recruitment and selection, job enhancement and promotion, and staff appraisal may seek to create checklists with a similar function to those used in colleges. The occupational standards provide one form of checklist against which a job description can be created, according to the level and responsibility of the post. Thus, for example, an employer seeking to appoint a middle manager within a firm may wish to use as a basis for the job the units of the Management I occupational standards for managers. These are:

- Maintain and improve service and product operations.
- Contribute to the implementation of change in services, products and systems.
- Recommend, monitor and control the use of resources.
- Contribute to the recruitment and selection of personnel.
- Develop teams, individuals and self to enhance performance.
- Plan, allocate and evaluate work carried out by teams, individuals and self.
- Create, maintain and enhance effective working relationships.
- Seek, evaluate and organise information for action.
- Exchange information to solve problems and make decisions.

Within the terms of the actual job that needs to be done, some of these may be seen as essential, others as desirable. The employer may be in a position to appoint a member of staff who does not currently have any experience in, for example, recruiting and selecting personnel. This could therefore be a 'desirable' rather than an 'essential' quality on the personnel specification. In addition, the employer may wish to make other stipulations about the personal attributes of the member of staff to be appointed – car driver, non-smoker, etc. – which can be added to the work-related criteria of the standards.

By using this method of recruitment, it becomes a simple step to use the 'unfulfilled' criteria of a new appointee as part of the staff development programme for that individual. In the example given above, staff recruitment and selection will become one of the priorities to be addressed by the individual without experience in this area. Completion of the outstanding units may lead to the award of the qualification, as well as promotion or a pay increase, thus enhancing motivation in the individual, in addition to providing a skills audit for the firm.

The Industry Lead Body occupational standards are not the only framework for describing work roles. Individual firms or organisations may wish to create their own standards according to their own product needs. The national standards do, however, provide a very useful starting point for anyone seeking to establish job descriptions for existing or future staff, and for planning staff development.

For the purposes of APEL, the essential ingredient is a known framework for the individual to work to in identifying current skills and how these can be demonstrated and used to the benefit of the learner.

Roles and responsibilities in relating skills to criteria

The learner will:

- identify the use to which identified competence is to be put through comparison with checklists of outcomes relating to possible qualifications or parts of qualifications
- decide whether to continue with the next stage of APEL, and gather evidence of competence, or follow a more traditional route to the desired outcome.

The counsellor will:

- ensure the availability of appropriate checklists that will help inform the learner of the potential pathways that identified prior learning can open up
- ensure that the learner has a realistic picture of how far current competence will lead, and whether APEL is the most appropriate route to follow.

The institution will:

- provide tutor time and accommodation for counselling and guidance.
- create and make available appropriate checklists against which the counselling process can be set.

Case study 2.3

Community Care Youth Training Induction

Twenty-eight students were enrolled on the programme, and as part of their induction week they were given an APEL interview. Two tutors were involved, and 40 minutes was allocated per interview. This was felt to be sufficient time, given that the majority of enrolled students were aged 16 and 17, and were likely to have little experience that could be accredited. Older learners would require a longer interview.

Both tutors followed the same interview format, going through the modules with the students and identifying those where accreditation might be possible. Modules where APEL was considered potentially relevant were identified by the tutors. These were:

- human development
- nutrition
- understanding caring for the elderly in an elderly persons' home or day care setting
- pregnancy and birth
- understanding disability
- awareness in caring for adults
- first aid
- basic home nursing.

Students were asked, prior to the interview, to bring with them any 'evidence' that they felt might be relevant to this vocational area – for example, current first aid certificates, GCSE results, childcare files, etc. In addition to matching these items of certificated learning to course modules, the students discussed fully with the tutor any voluntary work or other experience that they may have had in the care field. This was all documented on their Personal Training Programmes.

A procedural guidance sheet was drawn up:

APEL SESSION

Tutor needs

- initial assessment sheets on numeracy and literacy
- a piece of writing from the students about themselves
- relevant modules
- file for student to put relevant modules in
- Personal Training Programme sheet.

Student needs

- relevant records and qualifications
- relevant work.

Procedure

1 Check trainee's records of achievement, qualifications and relevant work and mark off relevant modules or sections of modules. If there is not enough time to do this in the initial session, this can be completed on review.
2 Put relevant modules in file.
3 Go through initial assessment sheets on numeracy/literacy and students' writing about themselves and discuss with the students any support they feel they need. Note this on the Personal Training Programme sheet if it is agreed.
4 Discuss trainees' relevant work/life experience.
5 Draw up individual programme on Personal Programme Sheet, including work placement and work experience, and modules and qualifications to be followed.

Conclusions

Although students of this age may not have as much 'prior learning' as more mature students, it was felt both by students and tutors that the APEL session was worthwhile. The students appreciated that certain aspects of the programme would not be a duplication of experience already gained, while the tutors felt that they were able to pick up on aspects of their students' learning that would not necessarily have been identified without these sessions. They could therefore plan and implement an appropriate course of study built around the individual students' needs and experience.

GATHERING EVIDENCE

This stage is the central and often the most difficult of the APEL process. It is here that the learner, having made a claim to possess areas of prior learning, and having expressed these as statements of achievement, gathers and presents the evidence that will support this claim. Documentation of evidence may take the form of a checklist of skills to meet a personal or occupational goal. Such a list may also be suitable for use on an application form where it is possible to stress and identify learning gained from experience rather than a statement of academic achievements. Alternatively, the outcome may be a more lengthy portfolio consisting of certificates, case studies, photographs, testimonials, reports, etc. which are assembled and presented to demonstrate and support the learner's claim to competence.

Portfolios fall essentially into two broad categories: the exploratory or self-orientated portfolio, and the specific or outcome-related portfolio. These differ in purpose, the first being very much of educational value through the process of its creation, and the second being created for a specific end purpose. There will be occasions on which the evidence incorporated in an exploratory portfolio is further selected and refined in order to create an outcome-orientated portfolio.

The basic format for both types follows a similar pattern. The starting point is a standard curriculum vitae, detailing schooling, work, qualifications and other achievements. This is then followed by:

- a statement of competences or skills claimed, matched to the outcomes for which the portfolio seeks to demonstrate competence
- a compilation of evidence supporting the claims to competence
- a plan of action for further learning or other activity (particularly in the self-orientated portfolio).

The precise form and content of the portfolio emerging from the preparation process will differ from learner to learner and will, to some extent, depend on the intended use to be made of the portfolio.

Self-orientated portfolio

This portfolio is an extension of the reflection process mentioned above, and covers all aspects of the learner's life and learning. It is typically the sort of portfolio that might be put together by someone thinking of returning to work, education or training after a break, or someone thinking of a career change. It is, in effect, the result of a process of examining the past to discover areas of hidden ability, and areas for further development.

The creation of the portfolio is in itself part of a learning process, and often one of the principal intentions is to convince the learner as much as any external assessor that competence does exist, and can be substantiated. Much emphasis is therefore placed on the act of its creation. As has been stated before, the exploration of the past and making sense of much of what it contains is not an easy process, and not one to be taken lightly by either learner or tutor.

Great benefit can be derived from supportive exercises that stimulate thought and analysis. Such exercises are often to be found in programmes designed to increase assertiveness, or in programmes used by careers guidance staff or counsellors. Typical among them are the use of the 'life line' to help identify where and how significant learning took place; the use of 'skills checklists' that ask learners to assess their own skills and identify where they have used them; matching identified skills to those necessary for work in defined occupational clusters.

The self-orientated portfolio gets its structure from the learner's sense of identity as defined in past, present and potential future activities. It therefore leads the learner to explore all areas of life, not simply those areas that are obviously work orientated. At this stage, the relevance of those periods of life during which skills have been acquired is not necessarily explored. The emphasis is on self and life experiences, and the learning that has accrued from them. It is therefore dealing with the whole self – weaknesses as well as strengths, but placing these in a context that leads to a positive interpretation in order to set the foundation for further development.

Purists will claim that the creation of this exploratory portfolio is not strictly speaking APEL, as at this stage the revealed skills it contains may not be presented for external assessment and accreditation. It is therefore perhaps more accurate to refer to this process as RPL (Recognising Prior Learning) or, as one college has chosen to do, call it IPEL (Identifying Prior Experiential Learning). It is, however, a process that many people need to go through in order to gain the confidence and develop the insight to create a portfolio of more specific, work-related skills for assessment and possible accreditation.

Through the Open College Network, it is possible for learners to receive accreditation for the process of creating a portfolio, and for the non-vocationally specific skills, such as communication or presentation skills, as demonstrated within the portfolio. The Open College Networks also provide a framework for accreditation of vocational skills, where occupational standards do not yet exist, or where there is no alternative appropriate qualification.

Portfolio preparation can be carried out either in small groups, or on a one-to-one basis. Both have advantages and disadvantages. Group work is cheaper to run in terms of staff commitment, but may inhibit those members of the group who need to explore sensitive areas of their lives, or who are unwilling to share their private lives with relative strangers. One-to-one is more expensive and may prove threatening to some learners. It also precludes the possibility of sharing experiences and learning from others. In an ideal world, it would be of maximum benefit to learners to offer a combination of both contexts.

At the end of creating this portfolio, the learner will have, in effect, an extended curriculum vitae, which documents learning experiences throughout life, provides evidence of how the skills claimed have been used, and begins to use these to define possible progression routes or frameworks for accreditation. It will close with an action plan, with a timetable for achieving long- and short-term aims.

It may be that the 'outcomes' against which learning is being matched in fact constitute the entry criteria for the next phase in the learning cycle. Thus the entry criteria for a particular course or programme of study may be defined in terms of a learner's qualities, abilities and aptitudes rather than the bland 'five GCSEs or equivalent' type of statement that has characterised many course entry criteria. It is essential that from this point onwards, the learner is clear about the criteria being worked towards, and therefore can begin to analyse which parts of the prior learning experiences are relevant to any potential future accreditation. The role of the APEL counsellor is of key import- ance in helping the learner decide on an appropriate framework in which to present evidence of learning and in making available a full range of options to the learner.

Outcome-orientated portfolio

This portfolio is essentially different from the self-orientated portfolio, and is usually created by a learner who has a clear goal in mind and who is using APEL to speed up the process of achieving this goal. It may be an extensive accumulation of evi- dence, or a simple record of employment, or a checklist of learn- ing achieved either within or outside paid employment. Its value lies principally in the portfolio of evidence or checklist of skills as a product demonstrating competence within the framework of a predetermined set of criteria, rather than in the learning processes involved in its creation.

This type of portfolio takes as its starting point the job or qualifi- cation that is being sought. It is a compilation of evidence of the learner's suitability or competence which is created strictly in order to match the criteria for achievement as laid down in the target framework. The desired outcome determines the structure of the portfolio. If a learner is seeking certification for an NVQ unit, the unit title and elements of competence are the targets and need to be stated clearly alongside the evidence, or proof, of competence.

Evidence can take many forms, and will vary greatly depend- ing upon the nature of the competence being claimed. Broadly there are two types of evidence:

- direct – created by the learner
- indirect – about the learner.

Direct evidence may include: artefacts, drawings, tapes, videos, spreadsheets – anything that can be authenticated as being the direct product or creation of the learner. Direct evidence is usually considered the most valuable type of evidence when it comes to assessment.

Indirect evidence may include: letters or newspaper articles about the learner, testimonials or references from employers, certificates, photographs or writing relating to something created by the learner. Most portfolios will contain a combination of both direct and indirect evidence.

A typical outcome-orientated portfolio will therefore follow a pattern that is something like this:

1 Contents page
2 Curriculum vitae
3 Statement about what the portfolio claims to demonstrate (e.g. NVQ units being claimed, ability to carry out a particular work role)
4 Cross-referencing index showing which evidence relates to which part of the claim
5 The evidence itself.

It is crucial that the portfolio is presented in such a way that an assessor can see clearly how the claim for competence is being supported, and how each piece of evidence relates to the framework within which the claim is being made. A very strong piece of direct evidence (e.g. a business plan or a complex artefact) will frequently serve to demonstrate competence in several elements, and possibly, several units. Claims to this effect must be clearly shown in the cross-referencing index.

The assessor must not be left to guess about why a certain piece of evidence has been included or why a particular element appears to have no evidence referring to it. It is the role of the APEL counsellor to support the learner through the process of identifying appropriate evidence and presenting it in a clear, logical, precise and relevant way. It is therefore essential that the counsellor is aware of and reasonably familiar with the occupational standards and any prerequisites of other targets against which the portfolio is to be assessed, such as a job description.

The amount of support given to a learner during the stage of preparing a portfolio varies greatly from institution to institution and from learner to learner. Most adult education centres, seeing the creation of the portfolio as potentially threatening and a learning experience in its own right, tend to give substantial individual and group support to learners. This stands in contrast to one former polytechnic which offers APEL candidates initial counselling and access to assessment, but provides no automatic support for the preparation of evidence of learning. The rationale behind this is that learners claiming skills worthy of accreditation at higher education level should be able to present a case that will justify their claims. In other words, demonstration of study skills and presentation skills is in effect seen to be a necessary part of the claim made through the medium of the portfolio. Under such circumstances, the use of a carefully prepared handbook to support learners through portfolio preparation may prove invaluable.

The amount of evidence that is necessary often causes difficulty. Just as NVQ units vary in size and complexity, so the evidence needed to demonstrate prior learning against the units will vary. Equally, employers or admissions tutors will need varying amounts of evidence to justify a learner's claim to prior learning. There is therefore no hard and fast rule about how many pieces of evidence are required per claimed competence.

Some NVQ standards stipulate a minimum number of observed activities in their performance criteria or additional guidelines for assessment. For example, the assessment guidelines in the first element of the Filing unit referred to previously state:

> If realistic simulation is the only method available, candidates must demonstrate competence by dealing consecutively with a minimum of twenty items to be filed, including the introduction of at least two files to the system and the need to seek guidance on non- and unclearly marked documents. Competence must be demonstrated on a minimum of three separate occasions, within realistically set time constraints. A completely different set of documents must be provided for each simulated assessment.

An APEL candidate would need to provide enough evidence to an assessor to convince that assessor that the above guidelines had been met. It is unlikely that any individual assessor would require a portfolio to contain three sets of twenty documents that have been filed in order to be convinced of a candidate's ability to carry out filing duties. Such guidelines are applicable on a college course preparing learners for assessment for an NVQ, or for a supervisor to assess in a work context. The most likely evidence presented by a candidate seeking accreditation through APEL would be randomly selected individual items for filing, with a written description of how these would be filed in the system familiar to the learner. Further evidence could be elicited by a short practical test, or through questioning by the assessor.

In the case of a learner coming from an unpaid work or domestic environment, the assessor will be looking for equivalent evidence of competence, such as a record of how new recipes are recorded and stored for future use, or how ongoing correspondence with outside agencies is kept and updated. A combination of the actual items and a narrative of how the system operates will provide the assessor with a sufficient range on which to begin to make judgements about the candidate's competence.

Although different awarding bodies offer qualifications incorporating the same NVQs, the stipulations about exactly how much evidence is required vary from one to another. Similarly, awarding bodies offering the possibility of APEL for qualifications outside the NVQ framework require differing amounts and types of evidence.

Where APEL is being used as part of an application for employment, an employer looking at a portfolio of evidence makes an informal assessment of the amount and quality of evidence presented. In this case, the evidence will have been put together in relation to the job description of the post being applied for.

The same principles apply to all these circumstances. The evidence must be clearly presented, well indexed, relevant, sufficient, valid and demonstrate current competence. These concepts will be explored in detail in the following section on assessment.

In all cases it is the responsibility of the candidate to gather or generate appropriate evidence for assessment. Portfolios, whether of the self-orientated, exploratory or outcome-specific variety, must be owned by learners as something they have created, and which accurately reflect their learning outcomes. The control that rests with the learner, and the fact that the whole process is one of openness, with no hidden institutional agendas, should build confidence in the eventual outcomes of the process. This is particularly important for those many adults who have a deep-rooted fear of any form of assessment, stemming from unsuccessful examination experiences at school, when they were tested more for memory and the ability to perform to time than for ability in the subject under scrutiny. The two types of portfolio described can therefore be compared as set out in Table 1.

Table 1 Comparison of self-orientated and outcome-orientated portfolios

Self-orientated portfolio	*Outcome-orientated portfolio*
Portfolio creation as a learning process	Portfolio as a product
Structured by sense of identity defined and extending through past, present and future	Structured by existing knowledge of job/qualification specification
The self is explored as a process for its own sake, including areas considered private	Presents aspects of self at present summed up to fit needs of job/qualification
Emphasis on life experiences, with focus on what has been learned from them without preconceptions about vocational relevance	Includes lists of competences and aptitudes appropriate to the job/qualification
Holistic	Specific to end purpose
All inclusive. May or may not contain materials that will be useful in applying for jobs or gaining qualifications	Edited for a specific purpose

Roles and responsibilities in portfolio preparation

The learner will take responsibility for:

- identifying and recording learning
- gathering and recording evidence of learning
- choosing a framework of outcomes against which learning and competence is to be matched
- reviewing the total evidence collected, and selecting appropriate items as proof of competence
- compiling a portfolio that demonstrates competence to the criteria of the target framework for assessment
- creating a cross-referencing index which demonstrates clearly

the relationship between evidence and the competence to which it relates.

The counsellor will:

- counsel the learner into group or individual portfolio preparation facilities
- guide the learner through the process of creating the appropriate type of portfolio, or moving from self-orientated to outcome-orientated
- be familiar with the outcomes framework of potential target qualifications
- liaise with appropriate assessors to establish precise requirements on types and quantity of evidence and any additional needs of accrediting or awarding bodies.

The institution will:

- create opportunities for group or individual portfolio preparation, through providing counselling staff and appropriate accommodation
- make appropriate arrangements with awarding bodies for the implementation of APEL in their awards
- ensure the availability of definitions of desired outcomes within each qualification offered to facilitate matching of evidence to assessment criteria.

Case study 2.4

Somali refugees

This work arose as the result of contact made with a group of women meeting regularly around a lunch club. They had had some input from a local college to help them improve their English, but this provision had finished. The outreach worker who was involved with the group felt that the members had skills which they had developed in Somalia, but which were not presently being used or valued because of the women's personal circumstances and their lack of confidence and English language skills. It was felt that the creation of a portfolio of prior learning could help these women recognise their skills, and help them plan ways in which they could begin to use them in Britain.

The first phase of the work involved working with four of the women who had the greatest English skills. They were supported in working through some materials that helped them create a curriculum vitae and document their experience and skills. The aims were quite clear:

- to build confidence
- to create a personal record of achievement
- to identify transferable skills
- to define options for progression
- to create evidence of skills for potential employers.

At the end of six two-hour sessions, these aims had been broadly achieved. All four women found the process a most rewarding experience, and their final portfolios enabled them to set targets for future development – ranging from setting up a co-operative, to seeking further English classes, and seeking employment in a hospital. These women requested that the other members of the group be given similar opportunities, which led to the second phase of the work.

The original four women, supported by a tutor, were paid to translate and adapt the material they had used for the creation of their portfolios, and work with the other members of the group in creating their own portfolios, in their own language. The aims of this phase were:

- to increase the confidence of the non-English speaking members of the group through identifying and valuing their skills
- to enable the women to identify and record skills for possible future accreditation, and to give a base for future work or study routes
- to create a model for development that could be used with other non-English speaking groups
- to create a set of learning materials for use by other Somali speakers.

Conclusions

The original materials used in the exercise were designed and written with a strong white, English cultural bias. They were found to be inappropriate in many cases, and raised a series of moral or religious questions in the minds of the women. There was not too much difficulty in identifying skills from education or work, as these could be seen as having tangible form and relevance in future paths. However, questions designed to help learners identify further skills that they might not have thought of identifying, and which started off with 'Can you . . .?' were answered at two levels – 'Yes, there is no moral or religious reason why I should not do this', and 'No, I cannot do this at present, as I have never had the chance to try it, but I could if someone showed me how to'. It is important that the design of materials to be used in future work of this kind takes into account the cultural, social and economic background of the client group.

There was also a concern amongst the group about whom the portfolio was for. Some of the women were unwilling to commit themselves to paper, having had previous negative experiences with officialdom.

Given the particular background of this group, there was a danger that reflection could lead to introspection and this could do more harm than good, if not handled extremely carefully. The use of group members in adapting the materials and facilitating the process for the non-English speaking members was extremely beneficial in making sure that discussion and personal exploration was kept within the bounds of what the learners could tolerate.

The exercise has shown that there is scope for APEL outside the context of demonstrating and describing skills through the medium of the English language, with the proviso that materials to facilitate the process are designed with specific reference to the cultural perspective of the target group. All the participants gained from the experience in terms of greater confidence, and the determination to build on their experience and use it as a positive element in their lives in Britain.

ASSESSMENT

Once the portfolio is completed to the satisfaction of both learner and counsellor, it can be submitted for final assessment. Final assessment is the process whereby the evidence presented by the learner is judged by an expert against the selected set of criteria, in order to ratify the claim to competence. There is no mystery about assessing prior experiential learning. All the traditional methods of assessment which have been developed over the years can be applied.

Positive outcomes from assessment may be entry to a programme of study, exemption from part or all of a programme, the award of all or part of a qualification, or access to work or promotion. This is, in effect, the 'crunch' time for a candidate as it is now that the preparation done in conjunction with the APEL counsellor or tutor is matched against the predetermined assessment criteria, and measured according to its validity, sufficiency, authenticity and currency.

Informal or verbal assessment is an integral part of the whole APEL process, as at each stage the counsellor and the learner together make judgements about the various aspects of the suitability of the route, the identification of skills, the type of portfolio to be created, the source and range of evidence to be gathered, and the format and presentation of the portfolio. However, at the end of process, the results will be presented to an external arbiter in order to judge the finished product. The criteria against which assessment is carried out are almost infinitely variable. NVQs provide a very clear set of standards and performance criteria for occupational competence, and many other awards are similarly detailed in their assessment and attainment criteria.

However, it is not only in the field of vocational qualifications that outcomes and assessment criteria should be laid down. Any tutor marking an essay, for example, has criteria against which that essay is marked. These may be, for example, demonstrated skill in presentation, content, discursive ability, sentence structure, research, etc. A marking scheme is then devised against these criteria, and all candidates measured against them. In a system of norm referencing, only a proportion of candidates will be able to achieve the top grade, regardless of the standard of their work. In a true criterion-referenced system, anyone demonstrating the sought-for skills can achieve the grade or qualification upon meeting those criteria. The major difference between non-vocational and vocational assessment is that in the former, much of the framework for measuring achievement is not written down, and so is open to different kinds of scrutiny from those used in awards that are competence based or outcome based.

In APEL, assessment should be a supportive process for the learner. It is not a rerun of the old school exams, where an unseen paper was completed to then disappear, never to be seen again, but resulting in a mystical mark or grade awarded according to some unknown marking scheme. This culminated in the issuing of a result denoting either a pass or a fail, a merit or a distinction. In the APEL system, the learner is fully aware of all the assessment criteria, and how these relate to the desired outcome of the portfolio preparation process. There is no mystery involved. This is not to say, however, that every APEL portfolio will always achieve what it sets out to do. There may be occasions when, despite careful counselling, the portfolio still fails to indicate with enough detail or clarity the competence claimed by the candidate.

In effect, then, assessment takes place at two stages: one informally, by the APEL counsellor or support tutor, who advises on the creation of the portfolio and its completeness and fitness for its purpose; the other more formally, by a representative of an awarding body, a prospective employer, or an admissions tutor in a college or other institution, who is ensuring that the evidence presented meets all the necessary predetermined assessment criteria. Part of the role of the assessor at both stages is to give feedback to the learner that will help in the formation of further evidence, or even just in a different way of presenting the portfolio in order to clarify and justify claims to competence where this is needed. Assessment is, therefore, not designed to allow people to pass or fail, once and for all, but will either endorse the claims made or suggest methods by which the claim can be further substantiated in a re-presented portfolio. There is no concept of 'failure' or 'missing the boat', because this particular boat does not move. It should be accessible at all times to the learner, with the gangway fixed and open.

The degree of formality of assessment will vary depending on the purpose of the portfolio. It will be aimed at ensuring fitness for the intended purpose.

Informal assessment

A self-orientated portfolio will probably be less formally assessed as its purpose is principally to assist the learner in the process of identifying and authenticating skills in order to establish appropriate and possible progression routes, including the creation of an action plan. The criteria for assessment will therefore rest upon the suitability of the action plan based on the evidence of learning demonstrated within the portfolio, and the confidence of the learner to carry out the proposed course of action.

In cases where Open College Network accreditation is sought for the process of creating the portfolio, the assessment will also ensure that the criteria laid down in the submission for recognition have been met. These may include the way in which the portfolio is presented, demonstrated study skills, ability to draw specific conclusions from generalities, or any other criteria perceived as helpful by counsellor and learner in the process of portfolio preparation.

A portfolio of selected evidence intended for job-search purposes will be assessed initially by the APEL counsellor to ensure its appropriateness for its purpose. Where a specific job description is the prompt, this will include making sure that the evidence presented matches as closely as possible the content of the job description. Any additional information will need to include a demonstration of awareness of the needs of the work with regard to areas where experience cannot be easily demonstrated. It is possible to create a more general job-search portfolio which is, in effect, an extended curriculum vitae from which evidence of particular expertise can be extracted as and when needed for a particular job application. This portfolio will be assessed mainly by the learner who is likely to be the only person who can judge whether it fairly includes all the facets that need to be represented.

A prospective employer receiving a portfolio in response to a job description will undertake a further assessment of the portfolio and of the candidate, probably through an interview, to ensure that the candidate has the appropriate personal qualities needed within a particular role within the organisation.

Formal assessment

In terms of a more formal assessment of a portfolio, for example, for the purposes of NVQs, the assessor will need to look at the evidence presented with regard to its

- validity
- sufficiency
- authenticity
- currency.

In addition, there is a requirement that the assessment process itself is seen as reliable.

Reliability

Reliability refers to the need to ensure that assessment is carried out to similar levels of consistency by a range of assessors. In the case of NVQs, this is relatively straightforward because NVQs are based on national standards, and therefore assessment starts from an agreed base. Assessment by standard tests, especially those such as multiple choice tests, gives a fairly clear assurance of a learner's measured outcomes against an agreed template of 'correct' answers. To an extent, NVQs give a similar fixed framework.

However, every APEL candidate presents a totally individual portfolio of evidence, containing different evidence demonstrating competence. The assessor's role is not only to match this evidence against stated standards, but also to apply the standards consistently between candidates and in line with decisions made by other assessors using the same standards.

The moderation and verification processes established by awarding bodies lay down as far as possible the quality assurance criteria for assessment of the varied evidence presented in an APEL claim. It is inevitable, however, that even with clearly defined standards, performance criteria and range statements, the ultimate assessment process for APEL, as with other assessments, is one of professional judgement on the part of the assessor, in balance with the standardisation made possible by a detailed assessment framework.

Validity

Checking the validity of evidence involves ensuring that it matches the purposes of the assessment. Does the evidence really demonstrate the competence that is being claimed across the required range? For example, the inclusion in the portfolio of a completed artefact may demonstrate the learner's ability to complete the object in this particular form, in this particular material. The assessor will need to be satisfied that the learner can also create the object under a range of different conditions, and out of different materials. The presentation of a simple cotton dress is not valid evidence of a learner's ability to make a velvet evening dress. The assessor may well need to employ additional assessment methods, such as oral questioning, in addition to assessing the evidence presented in a portfolio, in order to judge the validity of that evidence.

There is, of course, no completely foolproof way of ensuring total validity in any assessment method. A single driving test is not necessarily the best way to judge whether a person will be a competent driver on another day, under different driving conditions. It is the job of the assessor to minimise the margin for error between what is presented for assessment and any possible misjudgement of the evidence.

Sufficiency

In addressing the concept of sufficiency, the assessor must ask, 'Is there enough evidence here for me to infer competence?' Quantity in itself will not provide the answer. Several pieces of similar evidence will still only demonstrate the same competence. A rough example would be that 15 letters asking for brochures will not demonstrate the ability to write and complain about faulty goods. The evidence therefore needs to be seen to cover the whole range of claimed competences in enough detail and variety to justify the claim for competence.

Authenticity

The assessor needs to be sure that evidence presented is genuinely the work of the candidate. Where evidence is the synthesis of the work of more than one person – for example, a firm's development plan – the contribution of the presenting candidate will need to be clearly indicated. It may well be that the portfolio is the only contact that the assessor has with the candidate, and it is therefore essential that its content can be ascertained as produced by that candidate. Such claims may be supported by indirect evidence from a supervisor or manager in order to enable the assessor to infer the authenticity of the claim. It is the role of the supporting tutor to ensure that such issues are addressed and clarified before the portfolio is submitted for final assessment.

Currency

The issue of currency is one of the most thorny in the whole APEL process.

A personal exploratory portfolio can identify learning contexts and the skills they have generated. A consensus on defining these skills can be reached by learner and counsellor together. However, if evidence is to be presented to an external assessor for accreditation, it may be necessary to demonstrate that competence is still current. There is no hard and fast rule about 'how current is current'. In areas where a knowledge or academic base is being assessed, then it may be possible to apply a longer 'shelf-life' to evidence than in areas where a practical skill forms the basis of the claimed competence.

For example, a 20-year-old degree certificate may still serve as evidence of a learner's academic ability to study, learn and evaluate, on the assumption that these intellectual faculties have been regularly used in the intervening years. However, a 20-year-old typing certificate may be of less value as technology, technique and business formats have changed over the period since the certificate was awarded. In order for this certificate to be accepted as evidence of competence, the assessor would need to be assured that the candidate had continued to type over the years, and was still able to operate at or around the level of competence assessed previously. In such cases, where hard evidence could not be provided, the assessor may wish the candidate to undertake a short test to ensure that competence is current. Some awarding bodies are attempting to overcome difficulties in this area by dictating a shelf-life – usually two or three years – for evidence presented in an APEL portfolio.

Assessor training

Assessment, in general, has no great mystique attached to it. College tutors, school teachers and trainers, undertake continuous, formative assessment with their learners, and administer summative tests at the end of a programme of learning. There is an argument, however, that says that assessment to standards requires a different set of skills from those already employed by teachers, tutors and trainers. Additionally, the skills involved in APEL assessment are different again.

There are several reasons for making this case:

- Standards are fixed and therefore allow no flexibility on the part of the assessor.
- Standards are about outcomes, and have no regard to 'process' or 'distance travelled'. They measure the end result of learning, not the means by which that learning has been acquired.
- Standards indicate that a person is competent. They do not say 'just competent', or 'more competent than average', simply that the person has proved ability to meet the industry definition of competence to perform in a given work role.
- APEL portfolios bring a wide range of evidence to be assessed, drawn from all walks of life. Assessors have to make judgements about stated outcomes generated in areas in which they, personally may have no experience, and relate these to the stated performance criteria.

These issues represent a huge departure from the content- or course-based structure within which most assessment has traditionally been carried out. Awarding bodies offering competence-based qualifications are now undertaking training for their assessors and verifiers that familiarises them with the different role of the assessor. The Training and Development Lead Body (TDLB) has produced standards for assessors and verifiers which form the basis of such training (see Appendix 3 for details of the Assessor and Verifier and APL assessor units).

Some Industry Lead Bodies (ILBs) are already insisting that only assessors who have been assessed to these TDLB standards can undertake assessment of qualifications incorporating their occupational standards. This stipulation will become the norm for all ILBs within the next couple of years.

Individual institutions of higher and further education will, additionally, continue to train and offer support for assessors appropriate to their own needs, and in accordance with their criteria for making awards.

Assessment methods

In some cases, the APEL portfolio may be the only contact the final assessor has with the candidate. In these circumstances, it is essential that the portfolio is complete and carefully presented, so that all the criteria with regard to validity, sufficiency, authenticity and currency can be clearly addressed in order for a reliable assessment to be made. In most circumstances, however, the assessor will be able to meet with the candidate and therefore be able to employ a range of interactive assessment processes. If these are used, it is important to see them as an additional method of proving competence, not as a substitute for the portfolio nor as a necessary additional hurdle for candidates to leap.

There are many options open to assessors in order to seek additional proof of competence.

Skills test

The assessor may feel it necessary to ensure the currency of claimed competence, and may choose to do this by arranging for a short skills test to be completed. This should be as non-threatening and supportive as possible for the candidate, and should not be presented as something that resembles a traditional 'end test' or exam.

Written test

There may be areas of knowledge that are not fully documented in the portfolio of evidence, and the assessor may wish to ask the candidate to undertake a short written test or even a more lengthy piece of work, in order to ascertain the extent of the candidate's abilities. One former polytechnic which has introduced APEL insists on a reflective essay as part of the portfolio presented by any APEL candidate. The use of written work to authenticate competence for NVQ purposes, however, should be used with caution – unless it is the candidate's ability to write that is being assessed. Assessment within the context of NVQs is essentially to decide on a candidate's ability to perform competently in the workplace, not on the ability to write about the skills necessary to do so. It may therefore be more appropriate to ask for further evidence from the workplace – an analysis of a work-based problem, or indirect evidence from a line manager or colleague – than to set a written 'test' in isolation.

It should also be borne in mind that many people wishing to progress through APEL may have been out of formal education, and possibly even out of work, for some time. Having to do a written test may be threatening to such people, and re-create the feelings of confusion and inadequacy that they felt in their school days. It is, under these circumstances, an inappropriate assessment method, and may present a new, artificial barrier to progression.

Observation

It may be possible for the assessor to observe the candidate who is claiming competence actually undertaking tasks from which their claim arises. For example, watching the parent of a disabled child will demonstrate to an assessor that individual's competence to meet the child's needs more clearly than any paper-based portfolio. Work-based observation – actually seeing the candidate operating in the normal work environment – is a quick and effective method of assessing competence, but is insufficient on the basis of a one-off event. For APEL candidates, observation is an additional, not a primary, assessment method.

Oral questioning

The most usual way for assessors to have their minds put at rest about any possible 'gaps' in the evidence provided comes from simply talking to the candidate. This should be a supportive dialogue that enables learners to expand on the evidence already presented. Assessors may, therefore, need some training in how to handle such sessions so that they can make suitable prompts to the candidate. For example, although many people find it difficult to say what they are good at, most can respond more easily to questions such as

- Why did that happen?

- Where did you learn that?
- What happened next?

This process is less threatening and quicker (and therefore cheaper) than any other form of additional assessment. It also has the advantage of keeping the candidate involved in the assessment process, rather than having assessment 'done to them' by an anonymous, distant figure of authority.

Topping up

Some candidates will be told after their portfolio has been assessed that all the criteria have not been met, or that there was insufficient evidence of competence for the portfolio to be presented for accreditation. This is not the same as failing! Under these circumstances, the assessor's report should indicate where the gaps lie. It is then up to the APEL counsellor and the learner to devise ways in which extra experience or extra evidence can be gained. This may involve a short input from college, more work experience, a further collection of direct or indirect evidence, or simply a reorganisation of the material within the portfolio to indicate more clearly how the evidence relates to the assessment criteria.

Roles and responsibilities in assessment

The learner will:

- present evidence of learning in a form that allows for assessment against a framework of selected criteria
- undertake to provide supplementary evidence if required by the assessor.

The counsellor will:

- offer support and advice in the final stages of preparation for assessment of the portfolio
- act as advocate, if necessary, between the candidate and the assessor
- advise, following the recommendation of the assessor, on any further work to be done on the portfolio should the evidence not satisfy some of the assessment criteria

- prepare the candidate for any supplementary assessment to be carried out – e.g. a skills test.

The assessor will:

- be approved and recognised as an assessor by the appropriate awarding body or the institution offering assessment
- be familiar with the outcomes framework against which the portfolio has been prepared
- be able to make judgements about the match between evidence presented and stated performance criteria
- undertake or arrange additional supplementary assessment if necessary to complement evidence within the portfolio
- make recommendations to the candidate on further work needed on the portfolio, if any
- give feedback to the candidate on the portfolio and any additional assessment procedures
- record in requisite format for the awarding body the final recommendation on the award to be made to the candidate.

The institution will:

- ensure the availability of appropriately qualified staff for assessment in a range of areas of competence
- make arrangements for assessment to be carried out as and when the learner feels ready to submit evidence for assessment
- establish a fee structure for assessment that does not disadvantage those candidates who are not in employment or who have to meet their own expenses
- register appropriately with a range of awarding bodies, and meet their criteria for APEL assessment.

Case study 2.5

Hairdressing

As part of the move towards offering National Vocational Qualifications in Hairdressing, one college recognised that there was a need to recognise the skills students were bringing with them when they started a course in college. The move to a unit-based curriculum, with end tests for each unit, gave a framework within which APEL could be applied.

Each student who claimed to have some previous experience of hairdressing was given first a practical assessment to determine the level of practical ability, and then an oral assessment and the unit end test to determine the level of knowledge achieved. From the results of these assessments, carried out over a period of six weeks, it was possible to prepare an action plan for completion of the remaining units. Further learning took place in practical workshops, supported by learning packages, some of which were specially adapted to enable their use by students with learning difficulties. The process was reviewed through weekly tutorials. A system of compiling individual marks on computer was established, enabling student achievement to be kept on file for years, thus giving the student the facility to return to study in the future, with verification of what had already been achieved.

During the first year in which the process operated, it attracted few students who were able to take advantage of the 'fast stream'. However, it is felt by the Hairdressing section that APEL is a positive approach for attracting experienced craftspeople back into college to gain national recognition and accreditation for experience gained in industry. The college is committed to an extensive publicity drive in order to make the facility more widely known, and is moving further towards the whole of the Hairdressing provision being run on the workshop model.

ACCREDITATION

Although it will not be the aim of every learner who undertakes the APEL process, some will seek accreditation for their learning. Accreditation (usually in the form of certification) is the final stage of APEL, and is the means by which formal credit, or measured recognition, is given to the learner.

For a learner who has prepared and submitted a portfolio of evidence, accreditation is the process whereby the judgement of the assessor is ratified by an external agency – usually an awarding body. From now on, the learner has no further part to play, as the accreditation process itself is largely a series of paper transactions between the assessing institution and the accrediting body.

There are a number of frameworks through which credit can be achieved, but generally accreditation, as distinct from simple recognition leading to exemption or advanced standing, is dependent upon the existence of an outcome-based or unitised qualification. Such frameworks for accreditation come in a variety of forms.

National Vocational Qualifications

As stated earlier, it is the NVQ framework that has brought APEL to the forefront in recent years, especially within the context of further education and employer training. NVQs are generated from Standards derived by Industry Lead Bodies, which represent an occupational sector. Through the process of functional analysis with respect to particular work roles, they produce a definition of competence for that particular role. These statements of competence are the national standards. They are described in terms of levels, from 1 to 5, indicating increasing degrees of responsibility and autonomy. They are presented in the form of a series of units which are subdivided into elements. Each element is further refined by performance criteria and range statements, and any other necessary guidelines for assessment. Defined combinations of units make up the NVQs themselves at a predetermined level. (See Appendix 1 for details of NVQ creation and structure.)

Units within and across NVQs vary in size as well as content. Units certificated by one awarding body are automatically recognised by another, should learners wish to transfer them.

The standards are presented by the Lead Body to the National Council for Vocational Qualifications (NCVQ), which will ensure the standards meet all the stipulated criteria for an NVQ before publishing them and enabling awarding bodies to incorporate them within their qualifications. One of the stipulations for acceptance of a qualification is that it should incorporate the facility for the accreditation of prior learning. The National Council for Vocational Qualifications does not award NVQs. It simply kitemarks those qualifications that incorporate occupational standards and meet the criteria for assessment of learners against those standards. The actual

awarding of the qualification is carried out by approved
awarding bodies.

These awarding bodies issue general guidelines on assessment
of NVQs, and the major awarding bodies also offer guidance on
the implementation of APEL processes within their qualifications. The publication of Training and Development Lead Body
standards for APEL assessors has, to some extent, pulled all the
awarding body guidelines together so that an assessor trained
and accredited by one body will be recognised as competent by
others. (See Appendix 3 for TDLB units.)

Business and Technology Education Council (BTEC)

BTEC has concern for the process of gaining competence as well
as demonstrating its achievement. It therefore sees APEL as integral to its qualifications as part of initial assessment and in the
creation of an action plan for further study. It is also of use as part
of the formative and summative assessment strategies within the
programme.

RSA Examining Board

RSA uses the acronym APA (Accreditation of Prior Achievement). It, like BTEC, considers the process to be integral to its
competence-based awards, and assumes that registered
centres are willing and able to offer assessment of prior
learning. In terms of NVQs, RSA does not concern itself with
monitoring the process of delivering a programme leading to
NVQ assessment of competence, but only with the final assessment processes. The accreditation of prior achievement is seen
as an integral part of the initial guidance and assessment
process.

City and Guilds of London Institute (CGLI)

Centres registered with City and Guilds to assess NVQs must
make separate submission if they wish to offer the APEL facility.
This is because CGLI hold the view that APEL assessment
involves different skills from the usual NVQ assessment process,
and their verification processes would seek to ensure that APEL
assessors have the requisite skills to undertake such work. The

introduction of TDLB APEL assessor standards may go some way to resolving this conflict in the future.

Vocational Qualifications (VQs)

The major awarding bodies also offer vocational qualifications outside the current NVQ framework. Increasingly, these are defined in terms of units and outcomes, rather than a syllabus of content. This is being done mainly in preparation for future conversion to NVQs once the framework is complete. APEL may be employed within these qualifications in accordance with the general guidelines on the subject issued by each awarding body.

Open College Networks (OCNs)

OCNs offer a locally administered accreditation framework for learning that traditionally falls outside the remit of national awarding bodies. They are linked through the National Open College Network, which defines and monitors quality assurance processes within and between OCNs, thus ensuring the consistent application of the credit framework.

OCNs do not award qualifications, but issue credit awards for identified learning within a recognised programme. These programmes originate with tutors who, with their learners, identify the proposed outcomes from a learning activity. These outcomes, which are specific to the target group of the programme, are identified within a submission for recognition, and are given a level and credit rating. Successful attainment of all the outcomes to specified criteria will result in the award of the agreed credits. (For full details of OCN recognition and verification processes see Appendix 2.)

Because they are derived from a 'bottom up' approach, and are created by tutors for and with specific target groups, OCN programmes can be designed to accredit both learning process and outcomes. They are thus invaluable in the field of APEL, since learners can receive credit for the preparation of an exploratory portfolio, as well as for the skills identified within the portfolio itself.

The status of OCNs as Authorised Validating Agencies for Access to Higher Education courses ensures that their credits, which may be used as part of a claim for APEL, can also be used for admission into higher education. There is therefore a logical link with the higher education CAT scheme.

The expected forthcoming agreement with awarding bodies regarding progression from OCN to NVQ also extends the potential use of accreditation through Open College Networks for learners wishing to take their learning forward into new areas through APEL.

Higher education credit accumulation and transfer

Most of the former polytechnics and some universities have the facility to offer APEL, largely owing to the development of internal modular course structures and the implementation of credit accumulation and transfer schemes. This work was underpinned by the view of the Council for National Academic Awards that appropriate learning, wherever it occurs, may be recognised for academic credit towards an award.

APEL may be used to provide credit towards the content of a qualification. It is a major feature of this CAT scheme that it gives credit towards a specific end target. The 'credits' are of no intrinsic value unless claimed towards an award. The role of APEL in this system is to accelerate a learner's passage through a course, make the timespan for the achievement of the complete award more flexible by accumulating modules, or to upgrade one qualification to another (e.g. HND to degree) by dint of presenting evidence from work or some other context.

In other words, unlike the NVQ structures, individual certificates of achievement are not awarded for parts of a qualification, and unlike OCNs, credits have no currency value in an open market.

Roles and responsibilities in accreditation

The learner:

- has no role at this stage of the proceedings, other than to await the results of all the hard work that has gone into preparing the portfolio that has been assessed.

The counsellor:

- will begin to help the learner think about and plan next stages in learning.

The assessor will:

- transmit the results of the assessment process to the learner
- submit the completed records to an appropriate awarding body for accreditation
- liaise with the awarding body verifier or moderator and retain evidence used in assessment for recommendations on the award of credit for perusal, if demanded, by the awarding body representative.

The institution will:

- ensure that there exist within its structures sufficient and appropriate accreditation frameworks to meet the needs of the diverse community for which it provides learning and assessment opportunities.

Case study 2.6

Access to supervisory and management studies

A three-month pilot was carried out to develop and test existing assessment strategies within the total marketplace, but with a particular focus on individuals working within the voluntary and community sector.

The objectives were to:

- group prepared modules of supervisory and managerial competences in a way that ensured individuals seeking accreditation for prior learning could obtain credit for qualifications in line with the Management Charter Initiative and the NVQ system, which would be acceptable for personal and career development
- develop informal assessment systems and procedures involving skills-competence-related audits, identifying suitable types of evidence to accredit competences however gained (home, work, community etc.)
- promote access to supervisory management competences, particularly for those groups traditionally excluded from the employer-controlled personal development systems.

The competences were grouped, and supporting sheets were prepared for learners on:

- direct and indirect evidence
- sources of evidence
- verifying evidence
- quality/quantity of evidence
- stages in the production of a portfolio
- assessment.

Six participants attended an initial group counselling meeting at which MCI and APEL were explained. The group consisted of:

(a) Female aged 25–35

A former student who had left a traditional college course before the end because of domestic circumstances. She was seeking a qualification based on her employment experience. She started to gather evidence of competence, but did not complete or submit for assessment, owing to pregnancy. She intends to continue, using APEL, in the future.

(b) Male aged 40+

A full-time employee with the Local Education Authority, based in the community. He did not complete compilation of evidence because of a change of work responsibilities.

(c) Female aged 50+

A community worker and school governor. She did not complete this APEL process because she discovered the RSA Advanced Diploma in the Organisation of Community Groups through discussions with tutors, and decided this was a more appropriate qualification for her to seek. She therefore used the evidence gathered during the MCI pilot in a portfolio to claim competence in the RSA diploma.

(d) Female aged 30+

A local authority community worker with an administrative background. She is also a school governor. She completed compiling evidence within the timescale of the pilot, and sought formal accreditation for one unit.

(e) Female aged 30+

A retail manager seeking qualifications to support her work experience. She completed the compilation of evidence and gained accreditation for one unit within the timescale of the pilot.

(f) Female aged 30+

A retail supervisor facing voluntary redundancy. She was seeking qualifications to support her work experience and to assist in future job applications. She completed eight of the nine units within the timescale of the pilot.

Conclusions

1 The process of identifying and presenting evidence was slower than had been expected, and the participants might have benefited from a support group where they could discuss ideas on appropriate ways of gathering evidence.
2 The indexing and presentation of evidence favours participants with administrative and clerical experience.
3 These participants readily accepted that they were responsible for the identification, collection and presentation of evidence, but this would not necessarily be the case with all learners, especially those with less confidence or used to traditional, college-based learning.
4 The participants all benefited from the analysis of their abilities and the identification of their skills. One participant obtained promotion, and found that the APEL exercise helped her with the selection interview. The participant about to leave employment felt she would have more difficulty in providing paper evidence of competence once she had left work.
5 The MCI language was difficult to understand. It was generic and in some cases industrially biased. The units relating to quality seemed to relate to a production line rather than to a human service. This made the standards difficult for community workers to relate to. A

considerable amount of tutorial time was spent on discussing the meaning of the standards, how to generate appropriate evidence, and appropriate assessment methods. These difficulties will reduce as tutors become more familiar with the standards and the range of participant experience being presented.

CERTIFICATION

The end of the line in terms of the mechanics of the APEL process is the issuing of some form of certification. This can only happen when a learner's portfolio or documented evidence has been assessed and recommended for accreditation. Certificates for NVQs or units of NVQs are issued by recognised awarding bodies; OCNs issue their own credit awards; higher education institutions will sometimes issue certificates or diplomas which may count towards a Bachelor or Masters award.

Roles and responsibilities in certification

The learner, counsellor and assessor have no role to play at this stage.

The institution will:

• establish mechanisms to receive certificates of achievement from the chosen awarding body, and make arrangements for these to reach the learner.

PROGRESSION

As with any educational process, APEL should not be seen as an end in itself, but as part of a process of open-ended progression. It is therefore important that the learner is given continued support, even after the assessment and accreditation stages, to make informed decisions about appropriate next steps in the learning cycle.

It is is not inconceivable that a learner will wish to undertake further APEL as part of the next phase.

Roles and responsibilities in progression

The learner will:

- spend some time considering the next stage to be undertaken in the learning cycle – for example, continue to complete a qualification for which partial accreditation has been gained; use the qualification as a springboard into a higher level of education or training; use the portfolio as evidence of vocational competence in job search activities or to seek promotion at work.

The counsellor will:

- counsel and support the learner in deliberations about where to go next
- make available a range of information about possible progression routes, including those that take place outside the institution in which the original APEL process has taken place
- liaise with other tutors or organisations with or on behalf of the learner, where this is a problem for the individual learner, and give feedback on results of such liaison
- ensure, as far as possible, that people who are likely to receive the learner for the next stage in progression will accept the evidence presented for its intended purpose
- inform the learner of any issues arising that make a proposed next stage inappropriate, including details of any financial implications of the proposal, the likelihood or otherwise of employment as a result of the proposed next phase, and further preparation that will need to be undertaken before the proposal can be implemented.

The institution will:

- provide sufficient tutor time to support the learner in reaching a sensible and attainable decision on progression
- make available a range of information bases which can be used by learner and counsellor together in reaching such a decision.

Conclusion

It can be seen from all that has been written in this section that the learner is absolutely in the centre of the APEL process. However, it will normally be very difficult for such a process to be faced unaided. It is therefore incumbent upon the institution offering the facility, upon the counsellor allocated to support the learner, and upon the assessor to address issues of how to carry out their roles effectively and efficiently to the benefit of the learner.

Chapter 3 will look in some detail at issues that need to be addressed by institutions considering implementing APEL within their provision.

Chapter 3

How can we make APEL happen?

WHERE TO START?

The different stages of the APEL process itself were described in Chapter 2, and the wider social and educational issues that have led to the current rise in interest in the concept have also been outlined. The big question remaining for all staff within education and training institutions, and, indeed, for employers, is 'But how do we actually make it happen?'

There are, inevitably, no easy answers to this question. If there were, there would be no need for the number of current development projects around the subject. In order to find some answers, however, it might be easier to start with a further series of smaller questions, the answers to which can inform the individual institution's development plan and strategy for implementation. It might be helpful to find answers to the following:

- Why are we considering introducing APEL?
- In how much of our provision do we want to offer APEL?
- Who are the students we wish to attract through APEL?
- Which staff do we need to involve within the institution?
- Who do we need to work with outside the institution?
- How do we resource the service?
- What ground work do we need to do before we start offering APEL?

There are no 'right' answers: each institution will have its own ideas. An incremental approach that allows APEL to be introduced gradually into the provision may well prove the most effective. However, a few markers are set out below that may help focus the mind on the issues surrounding each of the questions above.

WHY ARE WE CONSIDERING INTRODUCING APEL?

There is a range of political, social and purely pragmatic reasons why colleges might choose to introduce APEL.

Equal opportunities

It has already been demonstrated that APEL is an integral part of a wide range of developments in post-compulsory education and training. One reason for this might be a sort of 'Heineken' effect – APEL reaches those parts that other systems cannot reach. This is a key element for any institution driven by a mission statement underpinned by a desire to achieve equality of opportunity, as well as one driven by the pressures of market forces.

The very nature of APEL enables the learner to identify a starting point for progression; moreover it places that starting point clearly in a meaningful context for the learner, with recognition for the means by which that point has been reached. Consequently groups that traditionally find it hard to enter the realm of education and training now have a real and personal 'entry permit' to a world that has previously seemed alien and hostile. Such groups include:

- *Unwaged women* who can have their time spent bringing up children, managing the home or caring for others recognised and placed in a vocational context of, for example, administration, management, caring or other occupations
- *Minority ethnic groups* who can build on skills gained within another cultural context to progress within the British system
- *Low-paid and part-time workers* who can use APEL to demonstrate their competence in order to seek promotion or new work prospects
- *Unemployed or redundant people* who can reassess the skills acquired in work to change careers or regain confidence and present themselves in a positive light
- *People with disabilities* who can use their successes in coping with an able-bodied environment to demonstrate skills and abilities that will enable them to progress.

Further and Higher Education Act

The Further and Higher Education Act 1 992 has made it clear that colleges must begin to operate in a way that provides flexible, high-quality and appropriate provision and that this is to be achieved in a climate of competition between institutions. Former polytechnics already have experience of life post-incorporation, but for colleges of further education in the maintained sector, this will create new challenges.

Traditionally, further education colleges have been the Cinderella of the post-compulsory education system, receiving relatively less funding and status than either schools or polytechnics and universities. Now they will be funded through Funding Councils that are removed from the local community that colleges seek to serve, and this bidding is to be carried out against criteria that are, as yet, still somewhat hazy. It seems likely, however, that they will rest on a combination of three factors: student numbers; in-college processes; and outcomes. There will be an assumption of expansion built into the formula.

Most of the provision currently offered by further and higher education institutions is already clearly eligible for funding under the provisions of the Act. However, there is a danger that some provision for adults, particularly part-time provision or that which may, indirectly, prepare adults for taking up education or training, may fall outside the remit of Schedule 2 if its precise role in providing access to accreditation or progression is not made explicit. College provision that can provide opportunities for accreditation or progression through APEL – from initial counselling through to vocational accreditation – may be seen as eligible for funding within one or several of the Schedule's specified 'courses', which are defined as:

- those leading to a vocational qualification approved by the Secretary of State
- those leading to GCSE, A Level or AS Level
- access to higher education, as approved by the Secretary of State
- a course which prepared students for entry to another course falling within the first three categories
- basic literacy provision
- ESOL
- basic numeracy provision
- in Wales, courses for proficiency or literacy in Welsh.

It therefore seems appropriate for colleges to explore the 'earning potential' of APEL through its ability to provide routes to recognised qualifications or progression within the terms of the new funding arrangements.

People, jobs and opportunity

In its White Paper of this title (1992), the Government has expressed its firm intention to enhance opportunities for training and education through the development of guidance and assessment services built on existing provision. An initiative is proposed that will:

- 'develop effective and comprehensive local information, assessment and guidance services for people at work'
- 'put people in the driving seat by offering them credits which they can use to buy the guidance and assessment services of their choice'.

The White Paper states that people will be helped:

- to identify their capabilities and potential and make their own decisions about future education, training and career paths
- to secure recognised qualifications, or credits towards them, for what they already know and can do
- to draw up realistic and achievable personal action plans for their future career development.

On the issue of making training credits available to more people, the White Paper also states that those given credits will be able to choose from a range of services including:

- information about occupations and the local jobs market (if appropriate)
- advice about education and training
- assessment and guidance to help plan their future development on the basis of their existing capabilities and potential
- counselling and advice about how to obtain qualifications, or credits towards them, on the basis of skills and knowledge that they already have (usually referred to as the accreditation of prior learning).

In order to maximise training, education and accreditation opportunities, colleges will need to be increasingly aware of such Government intentions, and adapt in order to meet them. The role of colleges has changed dramatically from the days when they provided full-time or day release courses and little else. They have the capacity, and the need, to become an integral part of a process of lifelong education that is relevant to all. The White Paper clearly signals the way in which development can happen – through partnerships, flexibility, and a structure built on guidance and formative assessment, rather one built on courses and summative testing.

In order to capitalise on these Government initiatives, colleges will need to extend and expand their links with local employers in such a way that they can provide education and training opportunities to meet the needs of the individual. A significant proportion of this expansion will place specific emphasis on APEL.

Resourcing

Increasingly, initiatives emanating from central Government and implemented via TECs, LECs, NCVQ and FEFC are looking at results (or outputs) as one of the means of allocating resources. Although there is a recognition by all concerned that the attainment of a qualification or credit towards a qualification should not be the only measure of a successful outcome, pressure is being put on colleges to provide access to approved accreditation and progression routes and this will support their claim for resources. APEL can provide a means of increasing numbers of learners seeking accreditation within an approved context.

An extensive project has been initiated in Croydon to examine the implications of outcome, or achievement-led resourcing, and practical methods of implementation. The need for such a project was foreseen as part of a strategy to create a flexible, post-16 provision.

A priority for development will be to move away from conventional post 16 educational costing and financial management based on the full time occupied place. Much more flexibility is required because new forms of client-centred and open learning can enable large numbers of clients to be served by an institution with a wide variety of unit costs. Establishing these will be a pre-requisite for sound institutional management, and for assisting the Authority to plan for increased client participation without automatically raising delivery costs. This is not to suggest that conventional full time study is not valuable, rather that alternatives are also needed. The portfolio of learning and delivery modes, together with their relative unit costs, available to the Authority will be a key factor in its future planning and budgeting.

(FEU 1990)

Although the role of the Local Education Authority with regard to colleges of further education will change from April 1993, the general issues raised by this project will remain pertinent. Calculating funding on the basis of full-time equivalent student numbers may become increasingly irrelevant, and other, flexible methods of accounting and allocating funds, based on meeting a wide range of learner needs through a wide range of methods, will need to be addressed.

All the above factors point to a number of reasons why colleges might consider implementing APEL. In fact, given the weight of pressure from outside and within the education system, it might be more appropriate to ask, 'Can we afford *not* to introduce APEL?'

IN HOW MUCH OF OUR PROVISION DO WE WANT TO USE APEL?

A college that is thinking about implementing APEL needs to decide how and where to start the process. There are a variety of options:

- offering APEL on a college-wide basis
- concentrating on an identified programme area
- concentrating on an identified course
- using APEL only in areas in which NVQs are available
- establishing a separate unit offering guidance and assessment on demand across a range of programme areas.

There are advantages and disadvantages to all these options, and all of them carry with them the option of starting small and allowing APEL provision to grow.

College-wide APEL

There seems to be little to recommend a wholesale reorganisation of the college simply in order to address the issue of APEL. However, those colleges that are undertaking change in structure and delivery systems for other reasons have found it logical to incorporate an APEL facility from the start. There is no doubt that using APEL brings with it considerable upheaval for staff and students, and the pace of change must be carefully judged and monitored in order to keep all players firmly in the game, and not tempted to take their bat and ball and go home.

APEL in a single programme area

Reorganising a whole programme area in order to offer APEL has the advantage of involving a team of a manageable size, with a range of specific expertise, across a particular range of subjects. Learners for whom APEL is considered appropriate can be offered a range of options within their chosen area, so that learners with different levels and combinations of achievement can be accommodated. If this option is chosen, it would make sense to select an area in which other key factors can be identified, such as

- availability of competence-based qualifications, so that staff do not have to start by writing their course or qualification outcomes
- easily identifiable target candidates, so that a pilot cluster can be brought in and accredited in minimum time for monitoring and planning purposes, and in order to disseminate success to the rest of the college as quickly as possible
- staff who are familiar with assessing to outcomes, so that initial staff training costs, both in terms of money and time, are kept to a minimum
- the potential for workshop-based delivery and assessment, to make it easier to free up staff for counselling and assessment duties, or where workshops already exist, thereby cutting the need for capital expenditure on creating one
- areas in which open learning is already established, so that there is a likelihood of some materials being available already for use in 'topping up'.

Examples of some vocational areas that meet most of these potential criteria for choice, and where success in implementing APEL has already been achieved, are: Hairdressing; Administration Business and Commercial; Management; Engineering; Construction; Access to Higher Education.

APEL in a single course

Starting with a single course or qualification has the advantage of involving minimum risk and financial outlay in order to test the practicalities of the system. It also involves a small number of members of staff who have established ways of working together as a team.

However, this latter point may also turn into a disadvantage as it may be hard to persuade such a small team of the advantages of changing their established practices. There is still, in many cases, the feeling that 'They can't be doing it right if I didn't teach them', and 'The only way to learn it is the way I learned it.' Such attitudes, which can be found in many college delivery teams, run counter to the idea of APEL, where a wide range of learning contexts is recognised and validated.

Restricting APEL to a single course or qualification also limits the potential progression routes for learners, by closely defining the context in which their experience can gain credit. This equally limits the perception of staff as to the range of possibilities for the use of APEL in a wider context, and may lead to the use of APEL as a post-enrolment means of gaining exemption rather than as a tool in pre-enrolment counselling.

However, if APEL can be established successfully within a single course, there is every likelihood that its advantages will be perceived by other members of staff, and it will thereby percolate through as desirable into other courses within the programme area. As in the above case of choosing a programme area as the starting point, the choice of course will need to be carefully made, so that learners can be recruited and successful outcomes achieved quickly.

APEL for NVQs

Choosing to start to implement APEL in a range of areas in which competence-based qualifications already exist is a very tempting option. It has the advantage of offering clear routes to accreditation, and, if NVQs or other 'approved' qualifications are chosen as the qualifications on offer, it may provide a basis for funding from the Funding Council. The existence of ready-stated outcomes for assessment purposes makes the role of assessor comparatively straightforward. In terms of targeting learners for

APEL, using ready-defined qualifications and standards makes it easy to market to potential learners likely to meet those standards, through liaison with employers and other members of the college community network.

However, even this approach is not without problems, as the availability of NVQs, although growing fast, is still patchy. In addition, the whole NVQ agenda is still subject to change as standards are revised, and awarding bodies enter or leave the field in particular areas or branch out from joint to sole accreditation. The assessment of core skills is still an unresolved issue for debate, as is the further development and implementation of General NVQs.

In order to provide maximum benefit to learners, therefore, colleges may wish to look in the first instance at NVQ areas, but at the same time ensure that other programmes and qualifications are also defined in terms of learning outcomes. This will enable the possibility of assessment and accreditation of not only vocational competence, but also other areas of skill where no NVQs are available as yet. A prime example of this is the area of Information Technology, where, although Standards exist, the full range of IT NVQs is still in the process of development. It is, however, possible to define, assess and record learner ability so that the learning can be used through APEL once the IT qualifications are established.

Establishing a separate APEL unit

Establishing a separate, free-standing APEL unit also has advantages in management terms. Such a unit may initially be resourced by top-slicing the budget or seeking external funding, after which performance targets may be set that will enable the unit to become self-financing or a minimum cost to the institution.

The size and scope of such a unit is variable. It may be a single entity, whose major purpose may be only assessment and accreditation. Staff within the unit may not necessarily undertake initial counselling, generic portfolio preparation and specific portfolio preparation with learners. This may take place elsewhere – in community centres, or within the context of college programmes. Alternatively, the APEL unit may become the hub of college-wide APEL provision, where all learners seeking APEL are referred, and where all their counselling, learning, assessment and accreditation needs are defined and met.

There are several advantages to a model based on an APEL unit. The unit can become the centre of all APEL work done within the college, but can operate alongside a more traditional college provision. In programmes in which competence-based qualifications are not yet in operation, the existing delivery systems can continue. The unit can undertake the marketing of its provision, and pursue liaison with local employers for either recruitment purposes or as part of a move towards work-based assessment supported by the college. A core staff can be recruited who will not necessarily be involved in activities in the main college programme. Costing and resourcing can be devised for the particular purposes of APEL, thereby avoiding the problems of a 'mixed economy' within the main college provision.

However, the major disadvantage of this model arises from the fact that it is all too easy to marginalise the APEL provision, which, it has already been shown, is integral to a whole range of good educational practices. A full-cost unit catering for the needs of employers and people in work would almost inevitably end up discriminating against people who could not afford to pay for the service, or who were seeking the accreditation or recognition skills gained outside of paid work. In the establishment of such a unit it would, therefore, be necessary to establish a pricing structure that did not preclude such people from using the system. It would also be advantageous to involve staff who are sensitive to and able to recognise the range of expertise being brought by learners, which may not at first glance fit neatly into a competence-based qualification framework.

It is very difficult to envisage a stand-alone unit that did not need to call upon college facilities such as open learning materials for topping up or supporting demonstration of competence, or careers and guidance provision. It is therefore essential that the whole college in some way 'owns' such a unit, by referring learners to it as and when appropriate, by being involved in the guidance, portfolio preparation and assessment processes, and by recognising the role of a separate provision over and above that played by more traditional course and workshop provision. In other words, a stand-alone unit cannot really be stand-alone. It may be separately managed and separately funded, but it has to be seen as an integral part of the college's provision, and not simply as a 'bolt-on' addition.

WHO ARE THE LEARNERS WE WISH TO ATTRACT THROUGH APEL?

As with any parts of college provision, there are different audiences to whom APEL may appeal. It will be helpful, therefore, to decide not only which parts of the programme will be organised to offer APEL, but also who the users of the service might be. There are a number of options, each requiring different responses from the institution in order to achieve them.

The most difficult model to adopt, but the one which best addresses issues of flexibility and equity, is one that is designed to offer the possibility of APEL to all learners approaching the college. This enables each learner, regardless of age, ethnicity or disability, to have access to guidance and counselling that will result in the identification of existing skills and planning of appropriate progression. The major implication of this overall targeting is that there must be a whole-college approach to developing APEL, in order to be able to meet the varied needs that will be identified through the process. There are, of course, advantages to this, in so far as it enables learners to have skills and abilities accredited in more than one area, or to have a range of accreditation options open to them. The disadvantage is obvious – a wholesale change in the way the college receives, initially assesses and provides learning opportunities for learners is time-consuming and costly. For this reason, it may not be immediately realistic to offer APEL to all comers, but to set this as a longer-term goal.

Mature learners on specific vocational courses are a readily identifiable group who will reap obvious benefit from APEL. It is relatively easy to establish counselling and assessment for them, as they already have an identified goal and predetermined outcomes for their course of study. Numbers will probably be small enough to handle without causing much disruption to current staffing or delivery structures.

Younger learners may also benefit from APEL, and increasingly have the advantage of bringing with them a record of achievement as a starting point for counselling and action planning. Some very successful work has been done with school-leavers attending a college as part of a Youth Training Scheme in Community Care. As part of their initial counselling and induction, they were given a checklist of programme outcomes, and many were able to identify areas in which they could already demonstrate competence. The effect was increased confidence in the learners, a clearer picture of what was to be expected of them, and a willingness to engage in the subsequent learning programme. Tutors, too, found the process of great value in helping them build relationships with their learners, and recognise their strengths from the outset. This model can be used for all programmes for which outcomes have been clearly identified, and the process for young learners could begin at a pre-entry stage while progression from school is being planned.

Unwaged and unemployed adults and young people alike will particularly benefit from the early stages of the APEL process, and the college may wish specifically to target these groups. This will require more preparation than targeting enrolled learners on particular programmes. The concept of APEL and its benefits will not immediately be known to the target group, and they are a dispersed group, thereby being difficult to contact and attract. The use of networks such as job centres, job clubs, adult education centres, and centres for unemployed people will greatly assist in reaching these potential learners. In order to avoid falsely raising hopes amongst this group, who are often already disillusioned by the education and training system, the college must be able to offer a range of accreditation opportunities, and the realistic possibility of progression routes, whether into education or training or employment.

Women are traditionally disadvantaged in education and employment, often having to return to the bottom of the jobs ladder after a career break. APEL enables the imbalance to be addressed and rectified, to some extent, by enabling rapid progression based on existing skills gained outside the paid workforce. Colleges may wish to target this group in the interests of equity and equality.

Similarly, minority ethnic groups may have skills that have hitherto been unrecognised or undervalued. APEL can uncover these skills and help these learners gain credit and credibility. In order to attract these learners, colleges will need to address issues of language and any cultural differences that could affect the process of identifying and valuing skills.

In aiming to attract learners with physical disabilities or other special needs, colleges will have to ensure physical access to the building, and the availability of counsellors who understand the particular needs, anxieties and abilities of this group. Physical access to assessment facilities, teaching workshops and other college services must also be addressed, along with a range of appropriate methods of assessment, which may be different from those for other groups of learners.

People in employment are an attractive target group as they may come sponsored by an employer, with learning that can be readily identified within a particular vocational area. It may also be possible to group learners with similiar employment backgrounds for portfolio preparation purposes, and carry out blocks of assessment for specified outcomes. There is an additional advantage in offering APEL specifically for this group, that arises from the possibility of workplace assessment. This may be carried out by a member of college staff, or by a workplace supervisor or assessor. This may reduce the amount of time and resources needed to establish simulations or other assessment processes or support portfolio preparation in order to gain evidence of prior learning.

In order for workplace assessors to undertake assessment towards qualifications accredited by an external awarding body, they, like college tutors, will need to seek appropriate recognised accreditation themselves. Some colleges, whose staff have already gained awarding body accreditation, are now offering training and accreditation through APEL to employers and their identified assessors.

The reasons for choosing to target one or more of these groups of learners will vary according to the location and type of institution offering APEL. It will, however, help to have a picture of who the learners might be whilst planning the provision.

WHAT GROUNDWORK NEEDS TO BE DONE BEFORE WE START?

Some colleges or other education and training institutions are not currently in a position to implement APEL, and may see a need to undertake phased preparation before being ready to do so. This will involve addressing the demands that may be put upon the system at all the major points of contact the learner has with the institution. It will therefore be helpful to look at the establishment of appropriate structures and processes for

- marketing, publicity and recruitment

- admissions and initial assessment
- induction
- on-programme support
- progression and exit.

Marketing, publicity and recruitment

In order to overcome some of the understandable scepticism and mistrust among staff that will probably accompany suggestions to introduce APEL, it will be helpful to undertake some internal marketing prior to advertising the facility externally. This will ensure college-wide awareness of APEL, and support for it in those areas where its introduction is intended. It is important to market APEL to staff as an alternative to more traditional routes to qualifications or parts of qualifications rather than as a total replacement for them. This is important whether or not it is intended to offer APEL in all areas of the college or only in specific areas, because working with APEL requires a general commitment to a flexible way of working with learners that cannot, in the long term, be contained within one sector of the institution. Thus a series of leaflets, brochures, in-house seminars and team meetings to describe the process and develop plans for implementation will prove as valuable for marketing internally as for attracting learners.

The numbers and type of learners recruited to the APEL provision will depend primarily upon the answers given to the questions posed earlier:

- Who do we want to attract?
- In how much provision do we want to offer APEL?

Marketing for recruitment can be directed at, for example:

- individuals from particular target groups (e.g. women, unemployed people)
- employers and employees
- the voluntary sector.

Whichever of these groups is intended for initial APEL targeting, substantial amounts of ground work will need to be done to raise awareness of what is still a new and relatively unknown concept. The problem with trying to 'sell' APEL is that although it is a straightforward idea, it represents a great departure from the traditional notion of having to go on a course in order to learn anything of value or to gain certification.

Successful marketing to employers has been linked closely to achievement of NVQs or other recognised qualifications. The heightened profile given to training by TECS, in the Investors in People and Access to Assessment initiatives, has led employers to begin to look seriously at the training needs and existing competence of their workforce. The progressive quest for quality through Total Quality Management or the attainment of BS5750 has also encouraged employers to look at present staff roles and development plans for the organisation. Some are looking at APEL as a fast and individually relevant route to a qualified workforce.

Colleges and training establishments are in a position to enter into partnerships with such employers by providing guidance to individuals, by participating in the creation of training plans for the organisation and for individuals in the workforce, and by meeting the training and assessment needs through work-based assessment, 'training the trainers', short courses, or open and distance learning provision. Marketing all of these facets of colleges' potential involvement with local employers can help to heighten awareness and appropriateness of APEL for sectors of society who have assumed their involvement with education and training finished some time ago.

Successful marketing strategies that have attracted members of the general public have included the widespread use of a consistent symbol in a variety of modes – the apple has inevitably proved most popular – sometimes accompanied by a tag such as 'Second Bite' to attract adults to return to education or training. General portfolio preparation programmes have been developed under titles such as 'Where Am I Now?', 'Where Now . . . Where Next?', or 'Making Choices', and have been given a high profile in college prospectuses and in separate publicity drives. These have drawn people who have felt themselves to be at a crossroads in their lives, and in need of the space for reflection and self-analysis that the first stages of APEL allow. Other slogans, such as 'Moving On', or 'Credit for What you Know' have attracted people with a slightly greater degree of self-confidence, who are ready to consider assessment of skills and competence almost immediately. These programmes have often had readily identified vocational links, with 'taster' sessions in-built for possible progression routes.

Whatever the target group for a recruitment exercise, it seems from the projects that have run around Britain that the most effective way of reaching the market is by word of mouth, while the least effective is the use of leaflets and brochures. Whilst these are certainly necessary as a back-up facility (to explain what APEL is and how it might work for individuals) most recruitment is achieved through press and radio coverage, open days, visits to the workplace, and seminars for employers and other professionals who may have contact with people for whom APEL could be appropriate.

Where leaflets and brochures are produced, it is preferable to avoid, or certainly minimise, the use of jargon – such as 'the accreditation of prior experiential learning'. The vocabulary is hard enough for professionals to grasp and understand, and is more likely to repel than to attract learners. More effective is a short phrase that is likely to attract attention:

- 'Are you an unqualified success?'
- 'Have you office experience but no certificate?'
- 'You don't need a course to get a qualification'

followed by one or two short examples of successful APEL candidates, and areas of life from which evidence can be drawn. This avoids the need to go into great depth about the process or the unwieldy vocabulary associated with APEL, and can be tailored to meet the needs of the target audience.

If APEL is to be restricted in the first instance to one particular programme within the establishment's provision, the facility can be included in the normal programme publicity. It can then be described in more detail as learners present themselves for interview for admission to the programme.

If APEL is to become a part of the overall provision, thought must be given to how learner enquiries will be received by the college. The first contact may be initiated from a variety of contexts, which are the basis of a series of flexible access points to the college – outreach provision of the college itself, other community-based initiatives, job centres, careers office, voluntary agencies, employment – and it may come at any time of year. Given the wide disparity of needs of learners from all these sources, the person receiving the initial enquiry – the receptionist, the switchboard operator, an admissions clerk, a tutor – will need to be familiar with the concept and availability of APEL. A standardised initial enquiry form will ensure that learners' details and perceived requirements reach the right person within the institution, whether this be an APEL counsellor or a course tutor. Such a form will also enable records to be kept for monitoring and review purposes, of the numbers of learners initially interested in the possibility of APEL, compared with eventual uptake of the facility.

Marketing, publicity and recruitment checklist

1 Do we have a target audience identified and a proposed means of reaching them?
2 Do we have supporting publicity:

(a) on the concept of APEL?
(b) on APEL within selected programmes?

3 Does the whole staff know about APEL and where it is on offer?
4 Do we have a standard first enquiry form so that we can monitor requests for APEL?
5 Do the reception staff know how and to whom to refer potential APEL enquiries?

Admissions and initial assessment

It has been found that one of the simplest ways of implementing APEL is as part of a process of initial assessment at the point of admission to the college. In order for this to happen, the entry points to the institution and the admissions process itself have to be addressed as a fundamental prerequisite of implementing APEL.

Many colleges are in the process of setting up, or have already established, an admissions unit, where initial guidance and assessment concerning the relevance, extent and appropriateness of APEL can be carried out. Such a unit is not necessarily a physical point within the college, although in some cases this is how the system is operated. The admissions unit represents more a cross-college function whereby the process of meeting the diverse needs of learners approaching the college can be initiated from their first contact with the institution. It will therefore call on the expertise of staff in all areas, from careers advisers to special needs tutors, from basic education to Access to Higher Education, from Business Studies to Engineering.

The good practice initiated in the admissions process should underpin the whole of the service that the learner will receive from the college, and be the starting point for student-centred action. As such, it will require a combination of guidance staff and administrative staff and have the facility to call on a range of specialist teaching and support staff across the institution.

The major advantage of operating such an admissions system is that it enables a centralised referral, recording and monitoring system to be established. Learners approaching specific programme areas often find themselves enrolled into an area of study because of the particular enthusiasms of the first person they encounter. The use of a generic counsellor as first point of contact minimises the risk of learners being enrolled into a programme of study that ultimately turns out to be inappropriate, thus running the risk of reinforcing the feelings of inadequacy and frustration that many adults experienced in their previous encounters with the education system. This first counselling interview should be carried out by someone who is as impartial as possible, and who is a disinterested party in the outcome of the interview.

One way in which a centralised admissions system can operate is to have generalist counsellors as a first referral point for potential APEL candidates. This counsellor (or team of counsellors) is placed at the hub of a fan-like structure, with contact points, through subject specific APEL advisers, into all programme areas where APEL is on offer, as illustrated in Figure 3.

It is the role of the generic counsellor to respond to initial enquiries from adult learners and to assess their needs through an initial guidance interview. A structured interview will not only help the learner decide on an appropriate destination and action plan for its achievement, but will also address areas of prior learning that can inform these decisions. A record of the outcomes of the interview will enable subject-specialist staff to have access to relevant information and also for the learner to keep and add to information given.

The form shown in Figure 4 is used by one college for all interviews with potential mature students. The form is printed on carbonised paper, in order to facilitate tracking of learners through the initial counselling and guidance stages. The learner

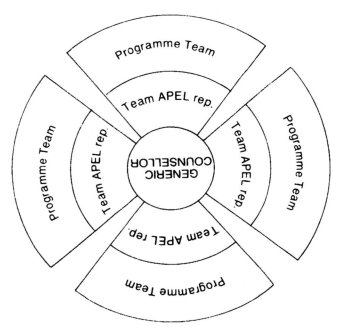

Figure 3 Relationship between generic and subject-specific counsellors

keeps one copy, the counsellor keeps another, and the third goes to the subject specialist to whom the learner is referred. From the APEL viewpoint, it is significant that the section on experience is addressed before that requesting details of academic achievement as this highlights the relevance of learning from experience.

During the course of the initial interview, it will be possible to ascertain whether APEL is an appropriate route to investigate – whether this is for the purposes of further exploration into needs and existing competence through a self-orientated portfolio, or as a rapid route towards assessment and accreditation. If the learner is likely to benefit from APEL, the counsellor can use qualification or programme outcome checklists provided by tutors and assessors to decide with the learner, in general, where existing competence may lie, and where evidence may be gathered to demonstrate it. This should include 'core skills' and study skills, wherever possible, as well as subject-specific knowledge and/or

Name _____

Address _____

_____ Phone _____

Aims (e g possible jobs. career changes study etc)	**Possible areas of study/training/ interest**
Experience since leaving school (e g paid work family voluntary work)	**Time available for study** (e g hours per week day/evening. school hours only)
	Any other limitations (e g travel. finance)
Achievements/Qualifications	**Possible areas of support needed** (e g creche. ESL. numeracy. mobility)

ACTION TAKEN
Qualification/Programme considered

_____

Possible APEL?   Yes/No
Units/Modules for APEL _____

_____

Enrolled/Firm offer made   Yes/No

Application form completed (Full time)   Yes/No

Creche form completed   Yes/No

Personal Tutor _____

Other action
(e g not enrolled. thinking about it further interview. referred to another person/college. finance discussions)

Staff Name   Date

Top Copy to enquirer Pink Copy to Course/Personal Tutor Yellow Copy to Admissions Unit

Figure 4 Mature student interview form

vocational competence. Where the level or range of competence lies outside the remit of the college, it will also be the role of the generic counsellor to advise the learner on more appropriate locations and/or qualifications. The admissions unit will therefore need to be equipped not only with staff who are competent in the role of educational counselling for adults, but also with a full range of careers and course information for use with learners.

The role of the admissions unit is principally one of initial counselling, informal assessment, and referral. If APEL is considered appropriate by both learner and counsellor, a specialist APEL counsellor is called in for the next stage. It is the role of this counsellor, who may or not be a specialist within a chosen programme area, to take the learner through a more detailed process of

- analysing where competence lies
- how it could be demonstrated
- preparation for the gathering of evidence for subsequent assessment
- planning with the learner any attendance foreseen as necessary to gain all desired parts of the chosen qualification.

At the end of this process, the learner will have a clear picture of the extent of possible APEL that can be claimed; how much work needs to be done alone, collecting together a portfolio of evidence; how much will be done in group or tutor-supported activities; how much will be done attending either taught components, or in open learning workshops. A provisional date for assessment may also be set. At this point, the learner may be 'admitted' to the individually designed programme that will lead ultimately to formal assessment.

Decisions must at this stage be documented, perhaps in the form of a learning contract betweeen the learner and the institution, wherein the mode of attendance and expectations on both parts are described, along with expected outcomes and a proposed timescale for their achievement. The admissions unit is a logical place for such records and learning contracts to be maintained.

The role of the admissions unit may therefore embrace more than a simple reception and referral function. It may become the interface between the learner and the rest of the college, and its functions may come to include:

- providing general education, training and careers advice and guidance
- initial identification and assessment of prior learning
- acting as a referral point to put learners in contact with relevant specialist staff, either within or beyond the institution
- helping learners to prepare individual action plans
- advising on appropriate and available learning methods (part-time attendance, open and distance learning facilities, etc.)
- liaison with childcare staff
- enrolling learners on programmes of study
- planning and initiating induction for learners
- recording enrolment, achievement, accreditation and planned further study
- advice on fees, grants and benefits
- general counselling.

The unit may also house support materials that will streamline the APEL system and reduce costly contact time between learner and tutor. These may include:

- self-assessment materials for learners
- expert systems for learner use to identify work aptitudes and training routes (e.g. ECCTIS, TAP, Adult Directions)
- programme and qualification entry requirement and learning outcome checklists.

The unit staff may undertake individual or group-based portfolio preparation of the exploratory type, prior to learner progression to outcome-orientated portfolio preparation and assessment by specialist tutors. They may also negotiate with employers regarding in-house training needs for employees and the college's role in meeting those needs.

In order to fulfil this wide range of functions, the unit will need to have an infrastructure that includes

- a process for receiving and referring initial enquiries
- a team of generalist counsellors and careers advisers with supporting materials, such as an initial counselling form, a copy of which can stay with the learner up to and beyond enrolment
- a team of specialist tutors who can advise and support learners in making choices as well as undertaking portfolio preparation work and assessment

- links into a college management information system that can track learners who, for example, choose a part-time route plus APEL through a traditionally full-time programme, and record units as and when they are assessed and awarded
- clerical support
- accommodation for individual counselling interviews and for individual and small group work.

These facilities should, as far as possible, be available at all times that the institution is open.

Admissions and initial assessment checklist

1 Do we have appropriate accommodation and support staff to establish a central admissions unit?
2 Can we identify appropriate staff to carry out initial guidance interviews?
3 Can we identify staff in each programme area where we intend to offer APEL, who can counsel and assess learners?
4 How can we establish a management information system capable of recording units as they are assessed and accredited?
5 What support materials can we provide to facilitate initial assessment, for example:

- self-assessment materials
- expert systems
- checklists of entry requirements and learning outcomes for programmes and qualifications on offer?

Induction

The creation of an admissions system that addresses APEL leads to the need to establish mechanisms for learner movement from the initial counselling phase into induction and on-programme support provided by the college. The overlapping roles of admissions unit staff and those involved in induction, teaching and assessing can be seen as a cycle that continuously addresses the progress of the learner. Co-operation and mutual understanding of all involved in the process are essential for the smooth operation of the cycle (see Figure 5).

The introduction of APEL into a learning programme may lead to a change in the structure not only of delivery, but also of the learner groups attending the programme. This can lead to insecurity both

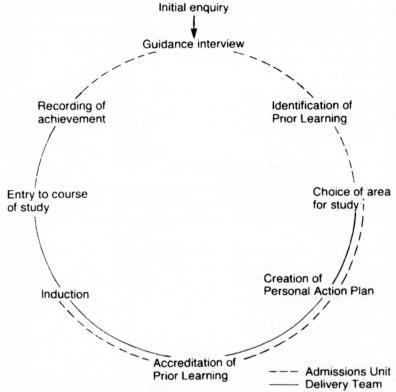

Figure 5 Roles of admissions and teaching staff

on the part of the learner, and of the staff involved in the programme. Learners are unsure of who their peers are, and tutors cannot easily identify and build relationships with a changing clientele, who attend only for tutorial support or for a short period of taught input.

It is important, therefore, for learners to be given a carefully planned induction programme that can prepare them for their particular learning experience. APEL candidates will already know from which parts of a programme they have potential exemption or accreditation. They will also know which parts of the programme they will need to attend and which parts they need to complete through self-supported study. For them, as for other learners, the induction process will need to cover all the normal college processes – geography of the buildings, library, crèche, catering services, etc. However, one resource that may not be available to APEL candidates but which is a built-in part of a full-time student's support network, is the continuous support of a peer group. Without carefully constructed support, a part-time or self-directed learner can easily become anxious and unable to identify sources for positive feedback. It can also be difficult to judge progress without other learners with whom to 'compare notes'.

The induction phase for these learners will, therefore, need to make clear the support that is available to the learner. This will include:

- time and place of any portfolio preparation groups that are meeting
- arrangements for tutorial support in evidence-gathering
- how to gain access to assessment as and when needed
- access to library and open learning materials
- information about possible progression routes.

Induction checklist

1 Will an induction programme for APEL learners need to differ from our normal induction programmes?
2 Can we ensure that staff will be made available to carry out induction at all times of the year, for individuals or small groups of learners?

On-programme support

Much has already been written here and elsewhere about the creation of flexible delivery systems in post-16 education and training. If APEL is to be incorporated, such flexibility is essential. Learning programmes will no longer be in the form of a continuous process starting in September and finishing in June, but will need to be available and responsive to the needs of a wide variety of learners approaching the institution at various times of the year. It is not, for example, helpful to a newly unemployed person approaching a college in February to be told to come back and enrol on a course in September.

A variety of internal structures are being developed to facilitate flexibility of provision. These include:

- *modularisation* of programmes to enable learners to attend selected parts of a whole programme, or spread attendance out over a timescale to suit the individual
- *open and flexible learning* to enable learners to use the institution as a resource, so that appropriate learning can take place at a time and pace to suit the learner
- *workshop-based provision* to afford the learner access to teaching and assessment more or less on demand
- *year round provision* to make learning and assessment opportunities flexible, and readily available
- *work-based assessment* to ensure that learners have the means of demonstrating competence in a real, rather than a simulated context, or by portfolio
- *short courses* to provide specific inputs needed by groups of individuals in order to start or finish a learning programme.

However, the above range of facilities that many colleges are introducing to support and provide for all learners are most effective if they are underpinned by support structures that make the institution a pleasant and practicable place in which to study. This is particularly necessary for adult learners, who have only their own motivation as a reason for returning to learning, and this motivation is often a fragile and easily destroyed entity. In addition, most adult learners are familiar only with a rigid, tutor-led education system, and may find it difficult to take charge of their own learning, and to acknowledge their ability to do so. The whole concept of workshops and open learning is therefore a greater problem for them than for the younger people who have come straight from schools where the self- or group-directed problem-solving approach has been the norm.

Some colleges have begun to find solutions to the needs of adult learners by the creation of an 'entitlement curriculum', which gives the learners 'rights' to support such as study skills, English and Maths, help with job searching, childcare, etc. This entitlement is underpinned by a comprehensive counselling and guidance service. This can operate successfully through a personal tutor system whereby each adult learner is allocated, on admission to the institution, a personal tutor who is linked to the area in which the learner is working. Regular contact may be maintained through timetabled meetings – e.g. weekly – or simply on demand by the learner.

The task for APEL candidates is even larger than for adults choosing to attend a whole course of study, as a greater proportion of their time may be spent in self-directed study. For APEL candidates, it will be the role of the personal tutor to ensure that deadlines are met for the presentation of evidence and portfolios, to give advice on the portfolio itself, where and how to gather evidence, and appropriate times, methods and frameworks for assessment and accreditation. It is important that the personal tutor is not the person who undertakes the final assessment, but is fully conversant with the assessment criteria against which the evidence will be matched. This will ensure the reliability and impartiality of the final assessment.

On-programme support checklist

1 Can we offer learning opportunities that are not bound by the traditional September to July academic year?
2 How many start points for programmes do we have in a year?
3 Can we offer assessment on demand through internal workshops or assessment centres, or through work-based assessment?
4 Do we have an entitlement curriculum for adults and does this include continuous access to counselling and guidance?
5 Does our current programme design enable learners to build a personal programme with in-built assessment and accreditation?

Progression and exit

Although APEL is often primarily associated with entry and initial assessment, it also has a place as a means of planning progression to another learning programme or to summarise accumulated learning prior to leaving the institution. The key, as always, lies in the learner identifying the purpose of going through the process of, effectively, updating the record of achievement and using this as the basis for planning the next stage in education, training or employment.

The counselling and guidance function should not, therefore, end on the completion of the learning programme for which the learner initially contracted with the institution, but should also be a part of the 'send off' given to the learner.

It is a fundamental principle of APEL that credit for learning, wherever and however acquired, is possible and desirable. Viewed from another perspective, it can be said that learners should have the 'right' to receive accreditation for what they know and can do, and that such accreditation will give them the currency for progression through a series of educational opportunities. In order for this 'right' to be taken up, it will be necessary for the whole of a college's provision to be recognised through an appropriate accreditation framework. This will create a map of the total provision, whereby the potential pathways to other learning, with identified levels and stated outcomes, will be readily available and identifiable to the learner.

Progression and exit checklist

1　Do we provide counselling and guidance to learners who have achieved their initial action plan?
2　Is all our provision accredited within one of the available frameworks in order to assist learners in planning and preparing for their next action plan?

Fees

If APEL is to become an integral part of college provision, the question of how to charge for the service has to be addressed. A number of models have been tried, based on whether APEL is to be implemented on the basis of full-cost recovery, as a loss leader designed to increase overall participation, or as part of the standard initial guidance and admissions processes for adult learners.

Most currently operating models offer an initial guidance interview free of charge, during which it is possible to assess the suitability of APEL for the particular learner.

Self-exploratory portfolio preparation workshops are often offered as part of community, adult education or access programmes, whether these are under the auspices of colleges or other establishments catering for the learning needs of adults. They are charged according to the non-vocational rates as applied locally, with appropriate reductions for unwaged learners.

Models for applying APEL in the context of vocational qualifications have been variously based on one of the following:

- an hourly rate, linked to the hourly rate for vocational courses, charged for the actual amount of tutor time taken up in portfolio preparation and assessment
- one or two block payments, calculated on the basis of an estimated average number of hours required for each stage to cover:

    (a) the counselling and support function
    (b) assessment

- free support in gathering and preparing evidence for assessment, but a set fee for each unit assessed (this is not the same as a fee for each unit accredited as assessment may not always lead to accreditation. However, the time spent in the assessment process needs to be paid for, whether or not the outcome is accreditation)
- a fee that is equivalent to the taught cost of each assessed unit, working on the basis that the saving to the learner comes in terms of a reduction in time needed to achieve a desired end, not in monetary terms.

The target group for which the service is being designed or made available will govern the amount and timing of fees charged, and the basis on which they are calculated. It may be desirable to have a banded fee structure designed on principles of 'ability to pay', so that a full-time employed person seeking accreditation for the purposes of promotion may be charged more than an unwaged person seeking accreditation for the same units for the purpose of gaining employment.

Whatever the structure and the precise amounts involved, it is important for the learner that the cost of the process is clearly identified from the point at which a 'learning contract' is established with the institution, wherein the outcomes being sought and the timescale and means by which they are to be achieved are clearly stated. There should be no room for confusion, and the overall maximum cost to the learner should not exceed the cost of achieving the desired outcomes through a more traditional, taught programme.

Fees checklist

1 How can we calculate the cost of the APEL service that minimises or eliminates loss to the institution, without dis-

criminating against learners whom we might want to attract through APEL?

2 At what point in the process should we start charging the learner?

3 Should we look at charging on the basis of

(a) hourly vocational rates – estimated or actual time taken;

(b) hourly non-vocational rates – estimated or actual time taken;

(c) a block charge per phase of the APEL process (e.g. initial guidance, portfolio preparation support, assessment);

(d) 'ability to pay';

(e) according outcome, as compared with the cost of achieving the same ends through a taught course.

Summary of college organisational preparation

In order to provide the possibility of APEL for a range of learners, colleges will need a range of facilities that are appropriate for the varying needs of different client groups.

- Learners who are unsure of their aims can be served by a range of self-assessment exercises and support in creating an exploratory portfolio to discover or recognise their skills, and to create an individual training or career plan. The resulting portfolio may then be submitted for accreditation.
- Learners who are unsure of their aptitude for their chosen aim can be served by self-evaluation and portfolio creation, and the opportunity to undertake short 'taster' courses or work experience in which they have the opportunity to demonstrate and receive credit for their skills.
- Learners seeking exemption or advanced standing need assessment and accreditation of current competence, skills and knowledge through direct assessment methods or a portfolio, set within the context of a proposed learning programme or qualification.
- Learners or their employers who approach the college for the express purpose of seeking accreditation need access to support in creating or gathering evidence and assessment through a portfolio of evidence, simulation or work-based assessment, plus any additional 'top-up' found necessary.

In order for any of these groups of learners to benefit from APEL, they will need continuous access to counselling, guidance and careers advice, and a range of frameworks within which they may receive accreditation. Flexible provision may therefore enable a college to provide accreditation opportunities for all its potential clients as demonstrated in Table 2.

Staff, curriculum and organisational development

Before APEL can be implemented on any scale, there needs to be a planned programme of development to prepare the institution and its staff. The creation of an organisational action plan, setting out precisely what is to be achieved, by whom and by when, will

Table 2 College organisation for meeting needs

Employer needs	College organisation	Learner needs
Audit of existing skills in workforce	Accreditation frameworks accessible through:	Initial and continuing guidance and counselling
	Flexible access points	
Creation of training plan	Initial and continuing guidance, counselling and careers guidance	Careers guidance
Work-based assessment		APEL
	Assessment workshops	Access to vocational qualifications
In-house training	Teaching workshops and seminars	Credit accumulation and transfer
Trainer training		
	Modular delivery	
Assessor training		Retraining and updating
	Open and distance learning	
Skills testing		Flexible learning opportunities
APEL	Short courses	
	Credit accumulation and transfer schemes	Education for leisure/retirement
	Portfolio development opportunities	Job search skills
		Study skills
	Work-based assessment	

greatly facilitate implementation, and provide a framework of objectives for the purposes of evaluation and future planning.

Academic staff development

It should be said that the introduction of APEL may create great insecurity for staff whose traditional role has been that of teacher. In a structure that offers a programme built around modules and other forms of flexible delivery, there is no such thing as 'my course' because the concept of 'the course' as a single entity with a fixed learner group and fixed entry and exit points is dying. Along with the demise of the course goes the concept of 'my students', as learner groups may vary from one module to another, and learners may attend partly during the day, and partly during the evening. Tutors used to recruiting for their own courses may find that they do not meet learners before they turn up in the classroom, or before they present a portfolio for assessment. They may be unhappy with the thought of generalist counsellors making initial judgements about learners intending to enter their field of study. Their own role as teacher may become replaced by one of workshop leader or work-based assessor.

It is not surprising, therefore, that many tutors reject the idea of APEL – not only because it may imply, in their minds, a reduction in the level of skill involved in their area, but also because it takes away from them the control that they are accustomed to have in their own domain. There are, of course, good reasons given why APEL is inappropriate in particular areas – there are no NVQs yet; the programme is based on a syllabus, not learning outcomes; the awarding body has not indicated that it will accept APEL; there is no time to cover the whole syllabus as it is, without taking staff away from the classroom for other purposes. All of these are valid objections, but may often be a smokescreen for fear of yet another reorganisation being imposed from above with no apparent relevance to current practice.

In order to minimise the feelings of insecurity and turn the introduction of APEL into a positive experience, a series of strategies may need to be employed. One of these is to make explicit, through the college plan for the development of APEL, what the institution's long- and short-term intentions are regarding the introduction of APEL and the philosophy underpinning it.

It may help to lend credibility to APEL in the minds of staff, to implement a structured programme of staff development, making sure that all staff development undertaken by tutors and administrative staff is recognised through some form of accreditation. Some of the existing standards – for example, in administration, management, training and development – may provide a framework for such accreditation. Working to these standards will clarify the full meaning and application of the APEL process. Alternatively, in-house programmes may be accredited through Higher Education CATs or the Open College Networks. Such recognition of the value of the programme will help staff feel that they, as well as the college and its learners, can benefit from the process.

APEL is all about recognising the role of learning from experience. It will be helpful to emphasise this aspect within any staff development events by building on the experience of the participants, and recognising their understanding of the issues. Staff development needs to be facilitated, not led, as most of the participants will be able to express realistic views on the implications of introducing APEL within their area of responsibility. In terms of the range of exercises undertaken by participants in order to test out the feasibility and practicalities of introducing APEL, it would be useful to make these as broad and varied as possible, so that a range of teaching, assessing and recording techniques that will be employed during APEL can be experienced and evaluated. These will include:

- role plays
- interviews
- skills tests
- simulation
- observation
- group discussion.

In order to help tutors realise the strengths of APEL and their own role within an APEL system, an overall staff development programme will need to address:

- what APEL is, and why and how the college proposes to introduce it
- how APEL could fit into different areas of the college's activities, both within the NVQ and other vocational contexts, and for people using APEL for diagnostic purposes

- the role of APEL in the implementation of an equal opportunities policy
- awareness of the learning needs of adult learners – which generally are different from those of younger learners
- counselling skills – to help learners recognise their own abilities and choose appropriate progression routes as a result
- establishing and working as part of a new team
- supporting learners in portfolio preparation
- how to define outcomes of programmes
- how to assess competence – as distinct from knowledge
- how to assess APEL portfolios
- how to define programmes in terms of modules or units
- differences in the delivery of modular programmes and the traditional 'continuous learning' course
- setting up and managing a workshop for delivery and assessment
- creating and using open and distance learning materials
- the use of a variety of assessment methods, both in college and offsite
- the role of liaison with employers and other external agencies in implementing APEL.

Many of these issues have already been addressed by managers of institutions seeking to establish flexible learning systems. Their rele- vance to the introduction of APEL is as apposite as to all the other issues of economy, equal opportunities, changing client needs, etc. that have brought the issues to the forefront over the past few years.

Non-academic staff development

Administrative and other support staff may also have problems adjusting to the demands of the new system. They, too, will need substantial support in adapting, and their own views on implementation strategies will be invaluable. Issues that will need to be addressed with them will include:

- what APEL is and how and why the college proposes to introduce it
- enrolment processes, which will need to change, so that learners can attend parts of programmes leading to qualifications instead of a whole course, attend portfolio development workshops and enrol throughout the year

- new fee structures to be introduced to cater for such variable part-time attendance
- recording procedures that can not only track learner attendance, but also record units achieved. Such procedures will need to be able to identify:

  ♦ units/modules available to learners, with appropriate coding
  ♦ prior learning identified, assessed and accredited, with appropriate unit codes
  ♦ learner certification
  ♦ learner personal details
  ♦ work placements
  ♦ work-based and college-based assessments
  ♦ learner attendance at college
  ♦ planned individual programmes of learning (by unit/module).

The above considerations raise a series of additional issues such as:

- How long will records be kept?
- Will they be kept manually or on a computer, or both?
- Who will be responsible for keeping them up to date?
- Who will have access to the records – academic staff, administrative staff, learners, employers?
- Administrative staff may also be called upon to have an increased role in counselling and advising potential students.
- Other support services will also be affected by the introduction of new learning systems and management.
- Crèche workers will need to address the issue of a flexible system that can cater for short-term attendance starting at various points of the year, and preferably available throughout the calendar year.
- Accommodation officers may be asked to find rooms for counselling, portfolio preparation groups or an influx of short courses for employers.
- Catering and cleaning services may need to operate different hours in order to meet the needs of an extended and more flexible college timetable.

Organisational development

The above staff development priorities will be framed within a college organisation that offers flexible learning opportunities that will support and facilitate APEL as a means of access and progression. APEL will thereby become one of a range of facilities and services on offer in a college that is moving the emphasis away from the current provision that caters mainly for young, full-time learners within a timescale dictated by a September to June academic year, to one that is responsive to a range of learner needs throughout the calendar year.

The new, flexible college will:

- be part of a network of flexible and local access points for learners
- give equality of opportunity to all learners
- provide year-round access to guidance, referral and enrolment
- assist in the creation and attainment of personal action plans for progression
- support preparation for assessment through identification and collection of evidence of learning
- provide access to assessment on demand, workshop learning and roll-on roll-off provision in an adult, learner-centred environment
- give learners a choice of learning modes, including classroom-based taught modules or courses, workplace assessment and open and distance learning
- identify entry requirements and achievements by means of learning outcomes, not statements of academic achievement
- support the development and assessment of core skills
- offer a range of potential progression routes.

In order to meet all these ends, some colleges have found it necessary to reorganise not only their delivery and administrative systems, but also the management structures of the institution, creating more cross-college roles, devolving management responsibility, and creating a 'flatter' organisational structure.

WHICH STAFF DO WE NEED TO INVOLVE WITHIN THE INSTITUTION?

It will be clear by now that introducing APEL is not a matter of involving one or two staff within the college, but may be seen ultimately as an integral part of an overall development plan for the whole institution. The precise number and range of staff involved will vary according to the college's decisions about the extent and type of the intended provision – whether to limit the service to one programme area or faculty; whether to restrict it to areas where NVQs are on offer; whether to offer the facility to all learners, all adults, or only those in particular target groups. However, regardless of the short-term approach to introducing APEL, it is likely that there will be few sections of the college that will remain unaffected in the long term.

Whatever the intended scale of the service initially, there are some minimum requirements for implementation, without which the process will not be workable. These are the identification of:

1 initial counsellors
2 general APEL advisers
3 subject specific APEL advisers
4 assessors manager(s) of the service
5 administrative and financial staff to cost and operate the service.

The first four of these categories may constitute a very small team, as the functions may be carried out by the same people in different circumstances, so that, for example, a catering assessor may also take on the roles of initial counsellor and APEL adviser. It is important, however, that the functions of the roles are seen as separate, and that assessment is kept distinct from the counselling and support functions. It should be a rule that the person assessing the portfolio is not the person who has supported the learner in his or her development. It may even be that some of the more general counselling role is taken on by administrative staff rather than tutorial staff, thus reducing the costs involved in introducing APEL.

It is perhaps worth stating here that, just as APEL is not the most appropriate route for every learner, so it is not necessarily a process that needs to involve every tutor within a college, or even within a programme area where APEL is being offered. Just as learners come with their own individual strengths, so do tutors. Some work well with groups, but find one-to-one work less fulfilling. Some can create innovative and non-threatening assessment environments, while others can create accessible and user-friendly learning packages. A college that seeks to build on the strengths of its learners should also seek to build on the strengths of its staff, and these will be just as many and varied.

APEL provides an opportunity for staff to explore their own abilities and preferred working methods, and use them to the best advantage of all involved. Such aspects will become apparent through a structured staff development programme that is built on the principles of APEL itself – of providing a series of frameworks within which personal experience and competence can be recognised and valued, preferably leading to accreditation.

There will almost certainly be learners who come to college seeking accreditation in more than one area. In order to meet the needs of such learners, it is important that staff involved in APEL operate as a team, both within subject areas and in a cross-college capacity. Within this team, one person will need to have responsibility for overseeing the progress of an individual learner, through liaison with all other tutors and administrative staff involved. This will include calculation and payment of fees, establishing a learning contract, registration with appropriate awarding bodies, access to individual guidance and portfolio preparation workshops, work-based assessment, and recording of achievement. Without this constant source of contact, it is all too easy for individuals to become lost within a system that is itself new and often untried.

It will be the role of the APEL manager to co-ordinate and develop the facility across the college, or those parts in which APEL is being offered. This will involve preparation of staff and systems in order to establish APEL as effective and efficient. The manager will be responsible for arranging appropriate staff development and liaison with other members of staff with cross-college functions, such as access, assessment, progression, flexible learning, guidance, marketing. Providing the level of staffing necessary to meet the desired outcomes of the APEL service will also be the responsibility of the manager, who will need to establish with the senior management team of the institution how the APEL service should be resourced.

It is for this reason that the involvement of senior management in the process of establishing APEL is quite crucial. An identified senior member of the management team with responsibility for APEL ensures that:

- APEL is included within the strategic planning processes of the college

- APEL is in a strong position to compete for resources with other, more firmly established parts of the provision
- APEL is signalled as a priority, to all staff, governors and other interested and involved parties within the college's internal and wider community.

As well as the academic side of APEL, there is a need to create administrative and financial processes to enable its implementation. This will require the involvement of the financial managers, planners and the team of administrative officers who record learner involvement within the college.

Staff involved in operating the switchboard, receiving initial enquiries and referring learners to appropriate channels for further advice and information need to have a clear picture of the facilities on offer, and who is the best person to answer queries. There will also have to be a fee structure that does not disadvantage learners seeking APEL from outside the context of paid work, and a clear understanding of the grants and benefits systems as they apply to individual learners. As with other college services, it will be necessary to build in as much flexibility as possible in order to minimise barriers to learning.

Some colleges are exploring the use of administrative or non-academic staff for the initial screening of potential APEL candidates. This reduces the costs incurred by using tutors for this purpose, and serves to create a whole-team approach to APEL by breaking down the traditional boundaries between the various sectors of learner services. In this model, tutors, counsellors or careers officers only become involved once the APEL route has been identified as appropriate and in the best interests of the individual, in order to undertake the creation and realisation of the action plan.

WITH WHOM DO WE NEED TO WORK OUTSIDE THE COLLEGE?

Not all the changes involved in the introduction of APEL relate to staff and curriculum development within the confines of the college. In common with all other college services, APEL cannot operate in isolation from the outside world, but needs to be part of a far-reaching network in which the college is involved. Keeping the learner and learner needs at the heart of developments, it will become clear that networking, collaboration and partnerships are key concepts if APEL is to open up new pathways. A range of agencies and organisations will need to be involved locally, regionally and nationally. These will include awarding bodies, the Employment Department, TECs, LECs, other training and education establishments, the Local Education Authority, voluntary bodies and individual employers.

Awarding bodies

NCVQ have issued statements and guidelines on the implementation of APEL (or APL) within the context of NVQs – what it means and the role it has to play within the NVQ framework. These have been adopted and adapted by individual awarding bodies, who have similarly issued guidelines on their requirements for the operation of APEL within their qualifications. These have generally proved helpful to education and training institutions.

However, there are still discrepancies between the various registration, verification and assessment procedures of the different awarding bodies, which at times can lead to confusion and complication, and may reduce the incentive to introduce APEL.

Qualifications which are unit based, and which embed NVQs, sometimes do so in such a way that the statements of competence and associated performance criteria are hard to disentangle from the other constituent parts of the qualification. This, too, is a disincentive to both learner and institution, as it may be simpler merely to run the course in the traditional manner. It would therefore be beneficial for colleges to work with awarding bodies in order to establish clearly and simply their requirements for using APEL as a means of gaining access to their qualifications, and to try and reach some form of standardisation on these requirements.

There is equally some discrepancy between the amount of evidence required by different awarding bodies in order for awards to be made through APEL, and the 'shelf-life' of such evidence in order for it to be accepted as current. This places assessors, tutors and individual learners under great pressure in trying to find the most appropriate awarding body with which to work. Whilst it is understood that any new system must be open to scrutiny which is at least as rigorous as the old system, the amount of rigour that has been applied to APEL has tended to detract from its potential benefits. As colleges and assessors become more used to the implementation of APEL, they may be able to influence awarding bodies so that locally administered quality assurance criteria for assessment are valued as highly as they are at present on established validated courses.

Employment Department, TECs and LECs

The establishment of links with the Employment Department and TECs and LECs has in the past produced pump-priming moneys for researching and initiating APEL, as well as the counselling and action planning base available through Initial Training and other employment initiatives. Without this funding, APEL would not have reached even the patchy development that exists at present. These organisations can also provide access to local labour market intelligence, including areas of skills shortage, which can inform college marketing and strategic planning.

However, in addition to their funding and intelligence role, the TECs have, through the Investors in People and the Access to Assessment initiatives, brought APEL to the notice of a broad range of people outside the traditional range of education and training providers. It will be helpful for colleges to tap into these informed networks, where expectations are being raised, so that emerging identified and potential needs can be met. Colleges have the means to provide quality training for and with employers and employees, but delay in selling their services to these clients could result in their losing their opportunity to do so.

Other training and education establishments

Colleges may want to enter into collaborative arrangements with other training and education providers in order to meet the needs of the widest possible client group. It may be possible, for instance, to establish a regional, centralised adult guidance and referral service. Such a service, jointly financed by TEC, colleges of further and higher education, private trainers, careers guidance staff and, possibly, the LEA could operate impartially to help individuals or organisations meet needs quickly and appropriately.

Other partnerships may also be possible, based on the franchising of a particular part of the service – for example, initial assessment, or particular units where it would be costly or inappropriate to invest in specialist equipment. In collaboration with institutes of higher education, further education colleges could offer an APEL service for Access students, if admissions tutors in the receiving institution could identify the skills necessary for an entrant to be admitted to a given programme. Furthermore, it may be possible for several institutions to work collaboratively on the writing of open learning or other 'top-up' materials, or to share facilities for assessment.

It is important for all providers to start talking in order to understand each other's priorities, needs and working methods. In this way, areas of overlap that already exist, or areas of potential mutual development, can be addressed in such a way as to minimise cost and maximise opportunities.

Employers

Most colleges have firmly established links with local employers who use their facilities for customised in-house training, or part-time, day or block release for their employees. These relationships can be further built on by colleges through:

- the undertaking, with employers, of an audit of skills that exist within the workforce in order to establish where APEL might be appropriate and where training needs lie
- offering guidance on individual training or development programmes
- the creation of an organisational development plan, building on the existing skills of the workforce
- the development of a recruitment strategy based on standards
- routes to qualifications through APEL or through training.

Colleges can undertake work-based assessment themselves, or become involved in the training of workplace assessors. Larger companies may wish to have within their own staff not only assessors, but trainers who can undertake to meet identified training needs. Colleges can have a role here training in-house trainers, not only in the techniques of training, assessment and APEL, but also in appropriate routes and qualifications to work towards.

Smaller companies may still choose to use colleges for their top-up training and accreditation processes as a cheaper option than undertaking this themselves.

Voluntary sector

There is also a large market for potential APEL candidates to be found within the voluntary sector. Much of what happens in industry and commerce, as well as in education and training, is mirrored by activities of voluntary bodies. However, because of their diffuse nature, and their relatively low profile and status, their importance is often overlooked.

The UDACE report *Learning in Voluntary Organisations* categorises the work of voluntary organisations by placing their activities into six 'orientations', according to their primary interest. These are:

1 *Interest groups* (e.g. model railway societies, language clubs, keep fit)
2 *Service groups* (e.g. Age Concern, Alcoholics Anonymous, Rape Crisis)
3 *Advocacy groups* (e.g. political parties, Greenpeace, Campaign for Homosexual Equality)
4 *Social groups* (e.g. old people's clubs, Mothers' Union)
5 *Community groups* (e.g. tenants' associations, community arts groups)
6 *Vocational groups* (e.g. unemployed workers' centres, small business clubs, industrial society)

Learning that takes place within the framework of these organisations may be formal – for example, based on teaching, organised discussion, involving assessment and certification. Alternatively it may be informal – for example, learning through practice and experience, and social interaction. In either case, the learning can be accredited through APEL, provided it can be identified and quantified within an accreditation framework.

Learners join vountary groups for a very wide range of personal reasons. However, the fact that learning takes place outside a formal or statutory education or training system need not hamper learners who wish, in due course, to have their learning validated and recognised towards future planned progression. Links between colleges and voluntary organisations can open up progression through APEL for all these learners.

Colleges can also undertake APEL with paid workers within the voluntary sector, many of whom have gained years of unrecognised experience. Volunteers also often go unnoticed, but can gain credit for the many activities that are undertaken for the organisation – from teaching to caring, from counselling to management. Links established between voluntary organisations and colleges can, through effective publicity, highlight the strengths of both organisations, and increase the flexibility afforded by the range of provision offered.

Adult education centres

If adult learners are not to be penalised by the post-incorporation structures that will apply to further education, it is essential that colleges retain and strengthen links with adult education provided by Local Education Authorities. The distinction that in reality is blurred between vocational and non-vocational education risks becoming sharply defined under the new funding mechanisms, and it will be all too easy for the LEA to cut the non-statutory 'leisure' provision for adults amid the pressures to provide more, for less money, within the statutory sector. Partnerships between LEA adult education centres and local colleges, which make explicit pathways for progression through APEL will help to ensure that adults do not get labelled inescapably as either vocational or non-vocational individuals, depending upon where they happen to enrol on a learning programme.

One of the major reasons why adult education is continually under attack is because it does not place emphasis on qualifications for paid work. What this perspective fails to take into account is the fact that less and less time is spent by individuals in full-time work, and for women, who make up some 75 per cent of adult education students, the years given over to full-time paid employment are often limited to that period between caring for children at one end of life, to caring for elderly relatives at the other. To make the assumption that time spent out of paid work, or in part-time paid work during the other periods, is not worthy of recognition is to devalue or ignore the true contribution made by such people to the fabric and economy of our society.

It is in the provision of flexible routes to accreditation for such groups as these that the Open College Networks have made a key impact. They have, for almost the first time, enabled accreditation to meet the needs of learners, rather than making learners fit a predetermined accreditation niche.

Adult education centres, which have a long history of working with learners from their own individual starting points, could extend their service by explicitly undertaking generic APEL counselling, and establishing potential accredited progression routes within and from their provision. Through such a linking APEL structure between adult education and further education in all its guises, those adults returning to education through adult education centres can find a means of having their experiences recognised and valued. At the same time, a pathway is opened up for access to work-orientated qualifications for those who may seek to progress down this route.

The kind of networking briefly described above between all agencies involved in or with an interest in the training and education of adults, in addition to those working with young people in schools or on training schemes, will help put the possibility of progression through APEL firmly on the agenda of learner-centred progression from work, home, community and leisure activities.

HOW DO WE RESOURCE THE SERVICE?

Many of the resourcing implications of implementing APEL have already been mentioned in earlier chapters of this book. APEL will require a reallocation of staff away from classroom-based teaching activities into counselling, guidance, portfolio preparation support, open and distance learning and workshop-based delivery, and college and work-based assessment. Support staff will also be affected, having to devise systems for calculation and collection of fees; continuous enrolment; recording learner attendance and achievement; allocation of accommodation for initial screening, assessment, teaching and counselling and support; childcare.

Materials will have to be created to market the service and recruit learners; to guide learners on using APEL in particular routes; to provide checklists of learning outcomes against which competence can be assessed; to provide self-assessment opportunities through paper- or computer-based systems; to guide and advise on the process of portfolio preparation and submission for assessment.

In the early stages of implementation, at least, these changes will have to operate alongside the traditional, course-based delivery systems currently in operation. Unless external funding can be acquired, strategies will therefore need to be devised that can free some resources from areas with potential spare capacity, in order to establish the APEL facility. This will not be easy, as it will be almost impossible to find an area of college that is not already operating flat out!

The newness of APEL and the fact that pilots have so far almost all been run using external moneys make it very difficult to assess precisely the cost of setting up an APEL facility. Certainly one of the criticisms that has been levelled at APEL is that it is an expensive way to operate. This need not necessarily be so, especially if full use is made of facilities that already exist within the college, such as workshops and open learning.

One pilot run by a college in Sheffield used the college's own administrative support staff as 'guinea pigs' in establishing and testing APEL processes. The intention was to combine the accreditation of evidence gathered from inside and outside the workplace, workplace assessment, and top-up training, in order to gain certification in the RSA Diploma in Office Procedures (now superseded by NVQ Level 2 Business Administration). The diploma consisted of 20 'tasks' (the equivalent at that time to NVQ units), each of which could be separately assessed and certificated.

Two college tutors were given five hours each per week for 24 weeks, in order to undertake the full APEL process, from marketing and recruiting, through initial counselling, to final assessment. During the process, each stage was documented and appropriate recording processes developed for use in subsequent APEL work. The 240 hours invested in the pilot resulted in the award of 68 certificates of achievement, distributed across five learners. Two learners gained the whole diploma. If all five learners had achieved all tasks, the total number of certificates awarded would have been 100.

Outcomes from the pilot in terms of materials were forms for the recording of initial guidance interviews, indicating where accreditation would be sought by APEL, where work-based assessment was appropriate, and where some extra learning was likely to be necessary, and a series of top-up exercises to supplement existing open learning materials within the college.

It is possible to compare the cost of this pilot with the cost of running a traditional, full-time course to deliver the same diploma. On the basis of an overall 15:1 student:staff ratio for 21 hours a week, over 32 weeks, the total tutor input is 672 hours. In the pilot, a total of 68 out of a possible 100 units were awarded from 240 hours input – giving an average of 3.5 hours input per accredited unit.

- On the traditional taught model, a 68 per cent success rate would result in $672 \div (15 \times 20 \times 68 \text{ per cent}) = 3.3$ average hours per accredited unit.
- A 100 per cent success rate, instead of 68 per cent in the APEL model would result in an average of 2.4 hours input per unit.
- A 100 per cent success rate in the taught model would result in $672 \div (15 \times 20) = 2.2$ average hours per unit.

It can be seen from this that the two methods present very similar figures of efficiency of tutor input but the APEL model figures include time taken for the development of procedures and documentation. Whilst the APEL figures will almost inevitably become less once principles and practice are established, the only way to reduce the average hours input per unit on the course-based model is to increase class size or reduce class contact hours.

The above figures for the pilot do, however, come with some provisos, which arose because of the specific remit and experiences of the operation. They serve to illustrate some valuable lessons that can be learned in implementing APEL. The first is that the initial publicity for the pilot actually attracted 26 candidates. All of them began the APEL process, were counselled, established the extent of APEL possibilities, and began to assemble portfolios of evidence. However, administrative problems in registration with the awarding body, and the external assessor's insistence on what the candidates considered an unrealistic amount of evidence, resulted in a 50 per cent drop-out several weeks into the pilot. Although the difficulties were later overcome, the candidates could not be persuaded to rejoin the scheme.

Although some drop-out is to be expected in any type of provision, the size of lost candidates in this pilot was disproportionate, and is unlikely to be repeated given that the 'teething problems' have now been ironed out. It does serve to demonstrate, however, the demotivating effect of building up false hopes. A disenchanted learner is a lost learner! Further reduction in learners also occurred later in the pilot, due to sickness and job changes, which are more indicative of reasons for learner loss in the real world of colleges.

On the 'plus' side, however, the fact that the figures quoted above include the time taken to counsel those learners who did not offer evidence for assessment, proves even more clearly the potential efficiency gains in using APEL. The figures also include time taken to prepare forms and processes for recording initial and subsequent assessment. Once in existence these need only be re-created in the event of a change in the standards for assessment. Indeed, much of the work that was undertaken arose from the delay in receiving the Cumulative Assessment Record from the awarding body, which provides the necessary format for documentation. Changes in registration processes have now reduced this time-lag. Also included in the 240 hours is time for the creation of exercises for top-up learning, or for demonstration of skills for which evidence could not be established either at the workplace or outside.

All the work carried out within the pilot was done on a one-to-one basis with candidates. Costs could be further reduced by bringing learners together for group-based guidance and support, and the use of self-assessment materials. As the tutors involved in the pilot were feeling their way in the process, they found that they at first devoted a great deal of time to the initial counselling session. However, once they became more familiar with the process and more confident in its operation, they found they could give a structured interview, establish areas for APEL, and give initial guidance on the collection of evidence all within the space of an hour.

Although these factors were significant in keeping hourly costs relatively high, there were other factors present in this pilot that were cost-limiting. Because of the nature of the target group, there was a high correlation in their experience, resulting in a relative homogeneity of units claimed through APEL, and sources, both work based and outside work, for evidence of learning. The fact that the pilot took place with staff within a college, where final assessment was carried out, meant that it was easy to negotiate and undertake both workplace assessment and access to open learning facilitites without additional expense.

The above figures serve to demonstrate that APEL, once established, can operate at least as cost-effectively as the traditional course-led pattern of provision. It should, at the same time, result in increased participation, faster achievements, and greater learner satisfaction.

The above pilot was carried out within the cushioned environment of an externally funded project. However, colleges without this luxury have to find ways of freeing up resources from within their own budgets. Different methods of finding resources for APEL have been used according to the scale of the initial APEL facility introduced, and whether a whole-college or part-college approach is envisaged. Some of the options available are:

- to top-slice the budget to create a 'development fund', for which departments/faculties/course teams can bid in order to pilot APEL
- to establish a separate budget for central services such as admissions and initial guidance and assessment, and ask department/faculty/course leaders to make staff available to fulfil these centralised functions
- to set target APEL candidate figures for departments/ faculties/courses or the whole college, costed at a level that will meet the real costs involved
- for each department/faculty/course team to allocate an amount of staff time to APEL activities based on anticipated or created demand.

There are a number of ways in which flexible use of staff can be used in order to keep the costs of implementing APEL to a minimum, such as:

- timetabling tutors into workshops where teaching and assessment takes place
- extending the college year so that more consistent and frequent use is made of staff and accommodation
- using support staff for some of the initial screening of learners
- switching moneys between budget heads in order to pump-prime the system.

MONITORING AND EVALUATION

The change in delivery structures described above will necessitate a revised system of monitoring and evaluation. It is clear that the notion of measuring economic efficiency purely through staff/student ratios is inappropriate for a flexible college built on the principle of meeting individual needs. A more appropriate system would be one based on case loads, along the lines of that which has been adopted in open learning provision. It may also be that the commonly adopted four ratios to determine efficiency:

1 students enrolled: target enrolment
2 students completing: students enrolled
3 successful students: students enrolled
4 students progressed: students completing

are also inappropriate, and other performance indicators to measure effectiveness and efficiency will have to be found.

In order to establish appropriate performance indicators for the implementation of APEL, it will be necessary to gather comprehensive figures relating to:

- the number of initial enquiries
- the number of learners following the APEL route
- the number of qualifications/units awarded through APEL
- other positive outcomes – e.g. work gained, entry to higher education, entry to learning programmes with non-standard entry requirements, progression to higher level programmes
- drop-out rates
- factors around 'value added' – the difference between a learner's starting point and attainments on completing the planned course of action.

These will need to be set against a calculation of costs incurred, which include all overheads of the provision as well as the amount of staff time allocated to:

- initial guidance
- portfolio preparation support
- assessment.

These quantitative results can then be added to the qualitative results of staff and learner satisfaction with the provision, in order to enter into a quality cycle that will extend and enhance the service.

Where APEL is intended to operate on a cost-recovery or profit-making basis, it will be necessary to build into the planning and accounting process target numbers of learners and a pricing structure based on the average number of tutor hours input, plus other on-costs.

Evaluation will also need to take into account staff views on the process as operated. Are they convinced of the value of APEL? Have there been unforeseen problems/benefits that can be taken into account in future planning? Was enough staff time allocated for each stage of the APEL process? What measures could be taken that would make the use of allocated time more effective?

Not until all these issues have been addressed will it be possible to calculate the true value of APEL, and to decide on its future role within the post-16 system.

Chapter 4

Conclusion

This book has drawn on the experiences of large numbers of practitioners attempting to implement an APEL service within colleges of further and higher education and adult education. There is no single method of applying APEL, and there are no magic formulae to make it happen painlessly and overnight. Perhaps the only universal guidelines are:

1 Be realistic about an agenda for action.
2 Take those staff who will be involved with you, and build on their experience.

There is no point in making a battle ground out of an issue whose underpinning philosophy is one of recognition of individuality and personal ability. The introduction of APEL should not disempower the staff involved in the process whilst attempting to empower the learners.

There follows an indicative, but not exhaustive, checklist that signals aspects of college organisation and responsibilities that could usefully be addressed prior to and during the introduction of APEL, whether on a part- or whole-college model. The chart invites commitment to the process of implementing APEL through the identification of individuals with key responsibilities at each stage of the learner's passage through the institution and in preparing the college for the provision of APEL. This record may assist in the process of planning, implementation and monitoring, and help to make APEL a positive feature of tomorrow's college.

A PRO FORMA CHECKLIST FOR ACTION

Issue	Addressed?	Person(s) responsible
Marketing and recruitment		
Identification of target group for APEL		
Awareness raising		
Liaison with external bodies		
Gathering labour market intelligence		
Publicity design and distribution		
Internal awareness raising and staff development		
Initial guidance		
Availability of appropriate staff		
Self-assessment materials and expert systems		
Entry and exit skills checklists for programmes/ qualifications in range of accreditation frameworks		
Availability of appropriate accommodation		
Initial assessment		
Availability of staff to undertake initial assessment to ascertain appropriateness of APEL		

Issue	Addressed?	Person(s) responsible
Admissions		
Receiving staff aware of availability of APEL and referral routes		
Management information system that can record units as they are assessed and accredited		
Continuous enrolment and access to assessment possible throughout year		
Portfolio preparation		
Availability of appropriate staff to support generic portfolio and specific portfolio preparation		
Availability of accommodation for 1:1 or group portfolio preparation support		
'Topping up'		
Open/distance learning materials		
Teaching workshops		
Specific seminars or short courses		
Access to individual modules/units of qualification		
Assessment		
Availability of trained and accredited assessors		

Issue	Addressed?	Person(s) responsible
Access to assessment workshops		
Access to assessment on demand and range of assessment methods		
Accreditation Range of accreditation frameworks and awarding bodies at different levels		

Appendix 1

The creation and structure of National Vocational Qualifications

The process of creating and accrediting a National Vocational Qualification is realised through the following stages:

1 The Department of Employment establishes an Industry Lead Body where one does not already exist.
2 Occupational areas within the coverage or scope of the Lead Body are mapped and roles analysed in order to produce a framework of occupational standards.
3 Standards are presented as units of competence, broken down into elements, which are further divided into statements of competence with associated performance criteria, range statements, and guidelines for assessment.
4 Awarding bodies adopt the standards, incorporating them into existing or new qualifications.
5 NCVQ 'kite marks' or accredits the qualifications, at one of the five levels within the NVQ framework.
6 Awarding bodies administer the award of qualifications based on valid assessments, and monitor and verify assessment to national standards.

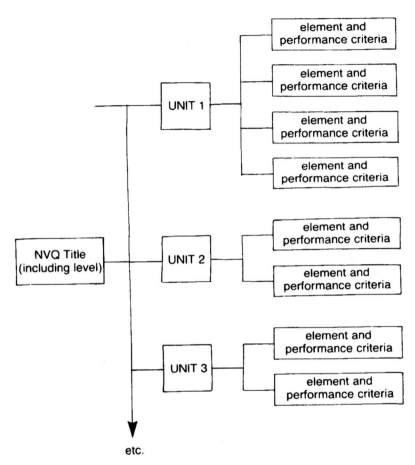

Figure 6 Sample structure of an NVQ

The NVQ framework for assessment automatically incorporates the acknowledgement and accreditation of prior learning, which is addressed before an individual training programme is designed for learners.

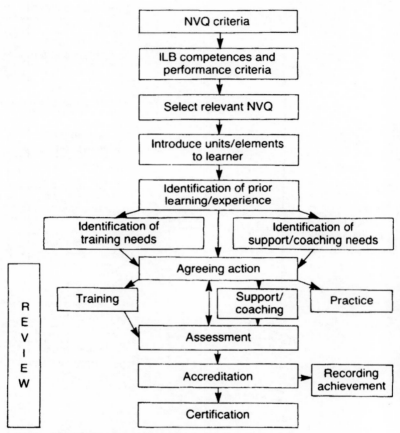

Figure 7 Flowchart for the award of an NVQ

Appendix 2

Open College Networks

Open College Networks is a generic term referring to Open College Networks and Federations, Access Federations and Consortia which are members of the National Open College Network, and therefore operate its agreed accreditation framework. This accreditation framework establishes four levels denoting stages of learning in accordance with agreed descriptors; an agreed definition of a credit based on 30 hours' notional learning time; processes of recognition through cross-sector, cross-organisation peer group panels; moderation of all programmes; mutual recognition of credits issued by all members of NOCN.

The OCN accreditation approach is fundamentally different from that of other awarding bodies in that OCNs primarily accredit programmes designed by tutors and trainers for particular groups. OCNs do not design and issue their own syllabuses. They encourage collaborative approaches to curriculum design across sectors and organisations. An important feature of the accreditation process is that it is carried out by peer group panels consisting of tutors, trainers and others with relevant expertise.

Programmes are reviewed, modified and recognised by the OCN through a process of recognition. Tutors are supported by an OCN development officer in presenting their programme to a panel of tutors experienced in the particular curriculum area. The panel reviews the internal consistency and coherence of the programme, addressing in particular:

- whether the programme is appropriate to the target group
- whether it draws on the values and experiences of the learners
- how it is organised to suit the target group
- how the content and organisation of the course relate to its aims

- how learners can be accredited for their achievement if they leave a programme before its end
- what will be assessed and by whom
- what criteria will be used to measure achievement.

The recognition panel agrees the level and credit values of the programme and identifies issues which need to be reviewed during moderation.

Moderation is carried out by independent moderators, who oversee a consortium of three or four programmes in similar curriculum areas. Samples of assessment from all the programmes are reviewed in the moderation process, and agreement is reached with the tutors on the award of credit. Recommendations for the award of credit, and for any refinements or changes to the programme, are made to the OCN by the moderator.

The process may therefore be seen thus:

1 Tutors design a learning programme for a particular target group.
2 Programme is presented to a recognition panel of experienced tutors.
3 Panel reviews programme, makes recommendations/amendments if necessary, agrees levels and credit values and identifies a moderator.
4 Moderator reviews operation of programme with tutors and learners.
5 Final moderation meeting samples assessments and agrees the award of credits to learners.
6 Learner is issued credits in a credit record. This includes details of the aims or learning outcomes of the programme followed and develops as a record of achievement.

(Adapted from Ecclestone 1992)

Appendix 3

National standards for assessment and verification

(Endorsed by the Training and Development Lead Body)

These units contain the agreed national standards for the functions of assessment and verification for NVQs and SVQs. They do not make up an NVQ/SVQ, nor is there any intention at present to have a full NVQ/SVQ in assessment. Some of the units are likely to be built into the NVQs/SVQs for professional trainers and supervisors, but most commonly they will be acquired as unit credits, in addition to any qualifications individuals may hold within their own occupational fields.

DESCRIPTION OF THE UNITS

Unit D32 'Assess candidate performance'

This unit provides the standard for the 'front-line' assessor who will normally be a supervisor or manager in the workplace, the trainer in a workshop, a college tutor or school teacher. The unit will also be suitable for the assessors of general NVQs. The assumption is that assessment takes place locally, primarily through observation of performance and examination of the outcomes of such performance, supported by questioning (oral or written) to assess underpinning knowledge and understanding. The potential demand for this unit will be considerable.

Unit D33 'Assess candidate using diverse evidence'

This unit is designed for the assessor who will need to draw upon a wide range of sources of evidence in making an assessment decision. These sources will include judgements made by other assessors, candidate and peer reports, candidate prior achievements and direct assessment as detailed in Unit D32. The 'second-line assessor' for whom this unit is intended will include those needing to assess more complex competences and the staff operating assessment services, in conjunction with first-line assessors. Candidates taking this unit should also gain, or have previously gained, Unit D32, as competence in direct assessment is assumed.

Unit D34 'Coordinate the assessment process'

This unit is designed for the internal verifier. This is a key role in assuring the necessary quality in assessment arrangements at local level. The functions covered include supporting assessors, co-ordinating the collection of evidence and undertaking internal verification of assessment practice. There may be one or more internal verifiers associated with an approved assessment centre, depending on the size and range of qualifications offered. Candidates taking this unit should have also gained Units D32 and D33 as it includes the functions of supporting and checking on the practices covered in the first two units.

Unit D35 'Verify the assessment practice'

This unit relates to the external verifier role. The external verifier provides a key link in the quality assurance chain, supporting and advising centres and reporting back to the awarding body. External verifiers are normally employed by awarding bodies to act as their agents. It would normally be expected that the external verifier was competent in the functions covered by the above three units.

Unit D36 'Identify previously acquired competence'

This unit is concerned with what is commonly known as Accreditation of Prior Learning (APL). It covers the activities of assisting individuals in identifying existing competence and in presenting themselves for assessment. This role is normally separate from that of assessing candidates, hence the creation of a distinct unit. The actual assessment, whether by APL or other means is a component of Unit D33, which people taking this unit would also be required to cover in addition to D32.

Table 3 TDLB assessor and verifier awards

Unit	Elements
Unit D32 Assess candidate performance	D321 Identify opportunities for the collection of evidence of competent performance D322 Collect and judge performance evidence against criteria D323 Collect and judge knowledge evidence to support the inference of competent performance D324 Make assessment decisions and provide feedback
Unit D33 Assess candidate using diverse evidence	D331 Determine sources of evidence to be used D332 Collate and evaluate evidence D333 Make assessment decision and provide feedback
Unit D34 Co-ordinate the assessment process	D341 Provide advice and support to assessors D342 Maintain and submit assessment documentation D343 Undertake internal verification
Unit D35 Verify the assessment process	D351 Provide information, advisory and support services for centres D352 Verify assessment practice and centre procedures D353 Maintain records of visits and provide feedback to the awarding body
Unit D36 Identify previously acquired competence	D361 Help candidates to identify current areas of competence D362 Agree an assessment plan with candidate D363 Help candidate to prepare and present evidence for assessment

Source: NCVQ (1992)

References and further reading

Notes on abbreviations: Council for National Academic Awards (CNAA); Further Education Unit (FEU); Her Majesty's Stationery Office (HMSO); Learning from Experience Trust (LET); National Council for Vocational Qualifications (NCVQ); Unit for the Development of Adult and Continuing Education (UDACE).

Adams, A., Brewer, M., Marshall, I., Tolley, G. and Whelan, T. (1991) *And It Must Count: Work-based Learning for Academic Credit in Higher Education*, London: LET.

Butler, L. (1991) *Unpaid Work: the Developing Potential for Accreditation*, London: LET.

Carroll, S. (1991) *Flexible Colleges*, London: FEU.

Challis, M. (1992) *Widening Access to NVQs: the Potential Role of Open College Networks*, Leicester: UDACE.

Challis, M., Edwards, P., McKelvey, C. and Wilson, P. (1991) *Two Urban Stories: the Development of APL in Newham Community College and Sheffield LEA*, London: LET.

City and Guilds of London Institute (1992) *Assessment and Verification Guidelines for Accreditation of Prior Learning*, London.

Ecclestone, K. (1992) *Understanding Accreditation*, Leicester: UDACE.

Employment Department (1990) *Accreditation of Prior Learning – a Training Agency Perspective*, London.

Evans, N. (1988) *The Assessment of Prior Experiential Learning*, London: CNAA.

FEU (1990) *Achievement Led Resourcing*, London.

Henebery, C. (1992) *The Assessment of Prior Learning and Learner Services*, London: FEU.

HMSO (1991) *Working Together – Education and Training*, London.

—— (1992) *People, Jobs and Opportunities*, London.

LET and County Avon Education Department (1987) *Handbook for the Assessment of Experiential Learning*, London: LET.

Mager, C. (1989) *Open College Networks: Current Developments and Practice*, London: UDACE.

—— (1990) *Open College Networks and National Vocational Qualifications*, London: UDACE.

NCVQ (1991) *Guide to National Vocational Qualifications*, London.

—— (1992) *National Standards for Assessment and Verification*, London.

Open University (1990) *APL: an Open Learning Pack for Advisers and Assessors*, Milton Keynes.

Percy, K. (1988) *Learning the Voluntary Sector*, Leicester: UDACE.

Simosko, S. (1991) *APL: a Practical Guide for Professionals*, London: Kogan Page.

Stanton, G. (1992) *A Basis for Credit*, London: FEU.

Wilson, P. (1991) *Resourcing the Flexible Curriculum*, Bristol: Further Education Staff College.

Woodrow, A. (1989) *Skills Assessment and Vocational Guidance for the Unemployed*, London: FEU.

Index

Lightning Source UK Ltd.
Milton Keynes UK
25 March 2011

169754UK00001B/2/A